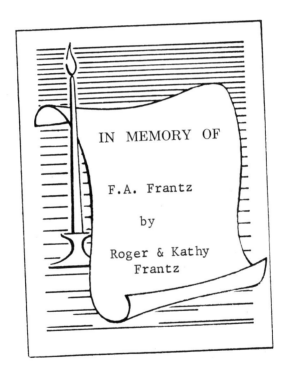

IN MEMORY OF

F.A. Frantz

by

Roger & Kathy
Frantz

The Calvary Christ

GERALD O'COLLINS, S.J.

The Calvary Christ

THE WESTMINSTER PRESS
Philadelphia

Published by The Westminster Press ®
Philadelphia, Pennsylvania

PRINTED IN THE UNITED STATES OF AMERICA

Library of Congress Cataloging in Publication Data

O'Collins, Gerald.
  The Calvary Christ.

  Bibliography: p.
  Includes index.
  1. Jesus Christ — Crucifixion. I. Title.

BT450.025   232.9'63   76-54973
ISBN 0-664-24801-2

For the Community at
Marymount International School, Rome

CONTENTS

Introduction   ix

I   Jesus the Martyr   1

II   Jesus on the Run   16

III   Crucified   40

IV   Agents of the Crucifixion   55

V   The Uncrucified is the Unhealed   70

VI   Atonement for All   92

A Personal Epilogue   115

Notes   *117*

Very Select Bibliography   *121*

Index of Names   *123*

INTRODUCTION

Can there be a temporary suspension of belief in the Resurrection in order that the full impact of the Passion and Crucifixion of Jesus may be experienced?

F. W. Dillistone, *The Christian Understanding of Atonement*

The true criticism of faith in the resurrection is the history of the crucified Christ. So we must subject belief in the resurrection to the history of the crucified Christ as its true criticism.

Jürgen Moltmann, *The Crucified God*

This book is a personal essay on Jesus' death – not a critical survey of theological opinions or a piece of detailed biblical exegesis. Too often a cloud of stale words covers Calvary. Theologians and exegetes can use a language remote from anything we feel. Conventional religious art asks for our conventional reaction. Tendencies towards evasion in all of us allow this art to continue and the dull language to grind on. We accept the old formulas, the familiar crucifixes and the ponderous pronouncements of scholars with a mixture of loyalty and mystification.

We need to find and fashion ways of reflecting on the crucifixion which can let it speak to us again with new power. To do this we may have to begin talking about other things. Our memory may need to slip backwards and forwards in time until it comes to rest on AD 30. Our gaze may have to glide around the world before it settles on Calvary.

To rush straight to the death of Jesus itself can prove a means for evading commitment. Instantly endorsing a well-worn theology of the cross may turn out to be no more than subscribing to some painless *theoria crucis*, which leaves us a long way from the *crucipraxis* or practice of Calvary. Acting on the words 'take up your cross and follow me' remains more valuable than interpreting them correctly.

Reflection on the violent deaths of committed men and women can offer us a way in. It is at least worth trying to let their stories evoke our wonder at the way heroic theory and practice can coincide. Hence the opening chapter. By recalling the fate of some warriors, assassinated leaders and martyrs, we may find that the crucifixion of Jesus strikes home with fresh force. His execution stands apart from the killings we will review, but the very differences can help us discover Calvary again. Contrasts let profiles emerge, and facilitate the search for meaning.

Once the opening chapter is settled, what follows? Let us take up in turn (1) the *story* of Jesus' road to crucifixion, (2) the *agents* of his execution, and (3) the *results* of that death. This amounts to examining the history, the causes and the consequences of Good Friday. For the history we draw on the gospel writers – especially on St Mark, the earliest evangelist. For sections (2) and (3) we can use St Paul, who in any case bypasses Jesus' path to death.

Paul never mentions the betrayal by Judas, the flight of the other disciples, the legal proceedings before the Jewish authorities and Pilate, and the place of crucifixion. He remains silent about the conflicts aroused during the ministry, the groups and individuals who emerged to menace Jesus and the attempts made on his life before the end finally came on Calvary. One thing blots out everything else for Paul – the crucifixion. Death constantly infiltrated the apostle's environment, but an execution by crucifixion – that hideous combination of impalement and display practised by the masters of his world – never proved a real possibility for Paul who was born a Roman citizen. His concentration on the way Jesus died let all the surrounding historical detail slip out of the picture. When he angrily demanded 'Was Paul crucified for you?' (I Cor. 1. 13), it was like someone today saying about a friend: 'He died on the electric chair', or 'they stood him against a wall and drove a car at him'. The sheer horror pushes other considerations away. One hardly needs to announce who 'they' were, or why he died on the electric chair. Likewise the mere fact that Jesus died by crucifixion filled Paul's mind with more than enough material for theological reflection.

Curiously the history of Jesus' road to Calvary can prove more troublesome than the theology of the crucifixion itself. Mark's simple-looking story may in fact bother us more than Paul's lofty meditations. The smoke of debates hangs in layers over Mark and the other gospel texts. We cannot be sure where the 'historical facts' end and the interpretations of the early church or the reflections of the gospel writers begin. Scholars can show themselves willing to exploit minor difficulties and differences in order to win a place in the biblical sun. Our problem in using Mark comes to this. On the one hand, the careful techniques of form criticism, redaction criticism and composition criticism[1] can be something of a trial and often a terrible bore. They may not only avoid the essential issues raised by the text, but also so pin us down to the pursuit of historical exactitudes that we may wonder whether exegesis can ever get us anywhere. At every point the exegetical ice creaks dangerously, as if it will not bear the full weight of even the lightest hypothesis. On the other hand, we need to remain at least within hailing distance of historical studies and critical scholarship. Otherwise we may drift away into a private world of our own, and ignore what we can truly learn about the road Jesus followed two thousand years ago to Calvary.

My proposal is this. Let us primarily take Mark's *story as story*. He wrote this gospel to frame the death of Jesus for believers – not as a work of 'scientific' history designed to please scholars. His story can come alive for us, if we allow ourselves to come alive in the face of his text. Any use of form criticism, redaction criticism and other techniques, which settles historical facts, speculates on developments behind Mark's text but fails to listen to the text as such, lets itself off easily and evades the challenge of his story. We would commit a similar blunder, if we undertook a quest for the historical Socrates, picked apart Plato's dialogues, argued that certain scattered sayings and episodes probably derived in some form from Socrates, but refused to let the *Apology* and the *Phaedo* in their entirety have an impact on us. Let us then read Mark's story as story. At points, however, historical questions will arise naturally and have their appropriate place. Without being tedious I plan to indicate – especially in chapters II, III and IV – the occasions when we need to enquire about the history of Jesus as such. At times we may allow ourselves to bring our historical questions to the crucifixion, provided this procedure does not thrust a knife through Mark's narrative, destroy the text by scholarly dissection and prevent the crucifixion from putting its questions to us.

Ulrich Simon has recently brought into the open what many have been thinking about much historical study of the New Testament. He contrasts 'the heights of scholarly ambition' with 'its diminishing returns'. 'There is certainly something ridiculous,' he suggests, 'in the fact that a fairly small collection of writings evokes so much learned comment with so little result.'[2] Simon's reflections serve to encourage a fresh approach. This book reserves a subordinate place for historical criticism, but refuses to allow that approach to be the normative and dominant method for dealing with Jesus' path to the cross. Taking Mark's story primarily as story promises to be more enriching than following the conventional path of much contemporary scholarship and engaging in (frequently) spurious quests for historical certainties and probabilities.

Our introduction would be misleadingly incomplete without one warning. This book will not have much to say about Christ's resurrection and his divinity. But I do not intend to doubt, let alone deny, either doctrine. Jürgen Moltmann correctly remarks about Christ: '. . . any interpretation of the meaning of his death which does not have as a presupposition his resurrection from the dead is a hopeless matter.'[3] Nevertheless, the death and dying of Jesus may come home to us in a more vivid and disturbing way, if we set aside for the moment the resurrection through which his divinity stands revealed.

Unless otherwise indicated, the scriptural texts in this book are taken from the Revised Standard Version of the Bible, copyrighted 1946 and 1952 by the Division of Christian Education of the National Council of Churches and used by permission.

In Australia, England, Italy, New Zealand and the United States I have talked with many helpful groups and individuals about material contained in this book. I am grateful to them all for their comments, contributions and encouragement. It would be a shameful omission not to single out for special thanks two Jesuit friends, Robert Faricy and Anthony Parish, who read nearly all the typescript and offered valuable suggestions. Finally, my warm thanks go out to Mrs Mary Bruce and Leonie Hudson who expertly typed the manuscript for me.

The Gregorian University, Rome   Gerald O'Collins
Good Friday, 1976

I

JESUS THE MARTYR

Even beasts must be with justice slain.

Andrew Marvell,
'The Nymph complaining for the death of her Faun'

Violent deaths have always played an enormous role in human affairs. We can trace and classify the victims right back through the centuries, till recorded history splits like quartz into the fragments of pre-history. Seemingly from the beginning the killing set in. Men, women and children have been clubbed, stabbed, stoned, burned, hanged, crucified, shot, beheaded, crushed between weights, torn apart on racks, electrocuted, poisoned, gassed, garrotted, blown apart by bombs and buried alive. The story of mankind has heaped high the instruments for violent death: the soldier's sword, the executioner's axe, the hangman's noose, the inquisitor's stake, the assassin's revolver, the airman's bomb, the cross for impalement, the piano-wire for strangulation, the shower-room for gassing. In his *Religio Medici* Sir Thomas Browne remarks mournfully, 'For the World, I count it not an Inn but an Hospital; and a place not to live, but to dye in.' Yet our world would lose its truly ghastly griefs, if it kept its hospitals but got free from death cells, extermination camps, napalmed villages, bombed towns, and battlefields of every kind.

The Bible hardly begins before Cain murders Abel – the first taste of so much killing to come. Violent deaths cram the pages of the Old Testament. Western literature opens with the skilled butchery of Homer's *Iliad*. From three thousand years ago we can still hear the crunch of metal on flesh outside the walls of Troy. It does not seem to matter much whether the images of violent death derive from man's undoubted history or from his literary imagination. The formal gap between fiction and non-fiction disappears. In a thousand ways human beings have proved themselves prone to seek out and destroy one another. The perspective of killing has helped to organize man's public existence and his private imaginings. The real world has created its make-believe counterpart, which reflects and sometimes encourages the relentless massacre.

On any reckoning Jesus of Nazareth belongs among the victims. He died by a particularly horrible form of torture killing. But how can we find a way to relate his end to the whole history of violent deaths? It may help to get things straight, if we begin with *individuals* who have died violently. Whatever we finally say about Jesus' role as representative man lifting his death to some universal significance, we must not lose our grip on the detail of the gospel narrative. A particular story led this known individual to a specific death on Calvary. Men stalked and killed Jesus himself. He was not just another soldier herded to death on the world's battlefields, not just another Jew trucked away to form part of the Final Solution, not just another victim of Stalin's insanity, not just another casualty after a bombing raid, not just another Vietnamese to die in a latter-day thirty years war. God save us from becoming inured to these modern versions of mass murder. They have created a fresh geography and history of savagery. Verdun, Nanking, Katyn Wood, Auschwitz, Stalingrad, Dresden, Hiroshima, My Lai – the names roll on reminding us that so far around one hundred million men and women have been killed in the twentieth century. Yet Jesus did not die as one of a large and anonymous crowd, whose butchery we can only mourn *en masse*. His killing left behind its own very particular scar in the memory of mankind. Both he and others interpreted his individual fate. He did not die a passive, silent victim – a mere entry in the rolls of an extermination camp, a cipher on an army list, just one of the estimated casualties after the devastation of a city.

When we begin to recall those who have suffered violent deaths, three groups offer a way in: warriors on battlefields, victims of assassination and martyrs. In that order they suggest increasingly useful questions and reflections about Jesus' own crucifixion.

Battlefields

First the warriors. Figures like Hector, King Arthur and Horatio Nelson arouse our sympathy and admiration when they die in battle. Wars always produce warriors who stay pinned to their posts as the enemy hordes close in, young heroes who press low-level attacks through a storm of flak; tank commanders trundling to death with their heads high above their turrets. This courage leaves its impression. Their names glitter like gold, defying us to disregard such glorious folly.

But we can only be left ill at ease, if we try to associate these deaths too closely with the execution of Jesus. Beyond question, some formal comparisons press themselves on our attention. Often these warriors had to struggle within themselves and win a victory on the inner battlefield before going out to face their foes. It was only after an agony of fear and indecision that they could leave their Gethsemanes and die courageously. They hoped to save others and, in fact, sometimes they succeeded in crushing the enemy. Their deaths can share a little common ground with Calvary. But we cannot move more than a step or two from this common ground without stumbling over major differences.

When Hector remained outside the Scaean Gate to fight Achilles, Priam's pleading caused no cracks in the walls of his son's determination. Finally the old Trojan king 'plucked at his grey locks and tore the hair from his head, but he failed to shake Hector's resolution'. Then Hecuba burst into tears, exposed one of her breasts and implored her son: 'Hector, my child, Have some regard for this, and pity me. How often have I given you this breast and soothed you with its milk! Bear in mind those days, dear child. Deal with your enemy from within the walls.'[1] The scene has repeated itself endlessly – parents pleading with their warrior-son not to risk his life.

But no such appeals reached Jesus on the eve of Calvary. Joseph had long before dropped out of the story. No grey-haired carpenter stepped forward to beg Jesus to shun danger – in this case by staying *outside* the walls of Jerusalem. Mary suddenly appeared among the women who witnessed the crucifixion (John 19. 26f.). But no gospel represents her struggling to hold her son back from his road to Calvary. When the gospels mention *her* breasts, it is to report how Jesus insisted that doing God's will constituted a higher value than the mother-son relationship. 'A woman in the crowd raised her voice and said to him, "Blessed is

the womb that bore you, and the breasts that you sucked!" But he
said, "Blessed rather are those who hear the word of God and
keep it" ' (Luke 11. 27f.). The gospels do not call on family
relationships to focus the horror of the crucifixion. Well before
that end they separate Jesus from his human home.

Jesus has no wife or child from whom to take a tender farewell,
as Hector does from Andromache and his baby son. Andromache
has lost her father, mother and seven brothers. She begs her
husband not to go: 'You, Hector, are father and mother and
brother to me, as well as my beloved husband. Have pity on me
now; stay here on the tower, and do not make your boy an
orphan and your wife a widow.'[2] Jesus, however, quite early in
Mark's narrative has moved in his own way both to resist the
sacrosanct nature of such natural ties and to establish a new
brotherhood and a new sisterhood.

> And his mother and his brothers came; and standing outside they sent
> to him and called him. And a crowd was sitting about him; and they
> said to him, 'Your mother and your brothers are outside, asking for
> you.' And he replied, 'Who are my mother and my brothers?' And
> looking around on those who sat about him he said, 'Here are my
> mother and my brothers! Whoever does the will of God is my brother,
> and sister, and mother' (Mark 3. 31–35).

In no sense do the gospels wish to present Jesus as bravely
breaking loose from the embrace of his family to face death – least
of all death as an heroic soldier. He extricates himself from their
circle long before the prospect of an ugly death confronts him.

The Christian tradition has, of course, from the beginning
picked up images of battle to interpret Calvary. Thus the ancient
Latin hymns frequently reach for the language of military
engagements. One thinks of the hymns with which Venantius
Fortunatus celebrated the coming of the relics of Christ's cross to
Poitiers (*Vexilla regis prodeunt, Fulget crucis mysterium* and *Pange,
lingua, gloriosi proelium certaminis*), as well as of the *Victimae Pasch-
ali*. This magnificent sequence shows 'death and life' fighting an
'extraordinary conflict (*mors et vita duello conflixere mirando*)'. In
the Anglo-Saxon religious poem, *The Dream of the Rood*, and other
medieval works, Christ appears not as victim or martyr but as an
heroic warrior whose endurance wins the day. At terrible cost to
himself, Christ the Champion gains his victory, despite the
apparent defeat of the crucifixion. Nevertheless, the gospel story
imposes severe limitations on the use of such battlefield imagery.
We will get into a mess if we fail to recognize how far the

crucifixion differs from deaths like those of Hector, King Arthur and Horatio Nelson.

In the *Iliad* a mightier warrior finally catches up with the young Hector. When Achilles draws near, Hector flees in terror before standing ground to fight and die. But no stronger man or superior force finally runs Jesus to earth. We would miss the point of his story, if we took Jesus to be a young 'prophet mighty in deed and word before God and all the people' (Luke 24. 19), who finally meets his match. Threatened with arrest, Jesus orders his disciples to show no resistance, and refuses to treat the conflict as a test of strength. 'Put your sword back into its place; for all who take the sword will perish by the sword. Do you think that I cannot appeal to my Father, and he will at once send me more than twelve legions of angels?' (Matt. 26. 52f.). Jesus freely surrenders. He does not meet his end because he proves too weak to defend himself or belongs to an outnumbered, outmanoeuvred or outgunned side.

The 'death' of King Arthur also leaves us a long way from Calvary. Sir Thomas Malory's account of the Knights of the Round Table slips away to a shining world of adventurous lords, enchanting ladies and picturesque castles. Love, faith and a hunger for hazardous adventure drive the knights on. Before King Arthur's final battle the dead Sir Gawain warns the king in a dream not to fight that day. But Arthur goes to the field. The fighting lasts all day, until by nightfall one hundred thousand men lie dead upon the ground. Only two wounded knights remain by the king's side. He catches sight of Sir Mordred, the villain who has caused all the evil. Arthur engages him in hand-to-hand combat, kills the traitor but receives a mortal wound. Mysterious ladies in black hoods arrive. They weep and shriek as they carry the king away in a barge to his presumed death.

In Jesus' case women abruptly come on the scene to witness his crucifixion and burial. But it is Pilate's wife, not Jesus himself, who receives the dream. When the governor sits on the judgment seat, his wife sends 'word to him, "Have nothing to do with that righteous man, for I have suffered much over him today in a dream" ' (Matt. 27. 19). No dream warns Jesus to take his disciples after the last supper, slip out of Jerusalem with them, and flee the conflict which faces him.

More importantly – the crucifixion does not occur after any kind of 'long day's fighting', which practically annihilates the forces of *both* good and evil. At the end, of course, Jesus himself stands more or less alone. But he does not come face to face with one deadly enemy, who has wickedly schemed to pervert the world but now has lost all his followers. Pilate is no Sir Mordred. He has neither provoked all the troubles nor seen all his supporters die. He simple despatches Jesus' case with the efficiency of a ruthless military administrator. Good Friday does not bring some public showdown with Judas. He glides away from the arrest in Gethsemane, repents his crime and hangs himself (Matt. 27. 5).

Even the devil fails to match Sir Mordred. In Mark's gospel Jesus shows himself 'the stronger man' (3. 27) – driving out demons and effortlessly overcoming the invisible powers of evil. But once the passion and crucifixion begins to loom up, the exorcisms drop away. Apart from the isolated case of one possessed boy (9. 14–29), we never hear of any evil spirits again. In Luke's passion story Satan enters into Judas (22. 3), Peter is warned that Satan wishes to 'sift him like wheat' (22. 31), and Jesus surrenders to those who arrest him: 'This is your hour, and the power of darkness' (22. 53). But any sense that Jesus goes to battle against demonic powers peters out at that point. John's gospel names Satan as 'a murderer from the beginning' (8. 44), who enters into Judas at the last supper (13. 27). Yet this 'entrance' is also Satan's exit from the story. Any pattern drawn from King Arthur's end will fail to fit. Jesus simply does not die in the twilight of his life, engaging some mortal foe in one-to-one combat – even a demonic foe. No gospel writer uses the terminology found in Ephesians 6.11–13, to describe the passion as follows:

> Jesus put on the whole armour of God that he might be able to stand against the wiles of the devil. For he was not contending against flesh and blood, but against the principalities and the powers, against the world rulers of this present darkness, against the spiritual hosts of wickedness in the heavenly places. Therefore he took the whole armour of God, that he might be able to withstand in the evil day, and having done all, to stand.

Brotherhood on the battlefield casts a warm glow over the death of King Arthur, Horatio Nelson and many other real or imaginary heroes. Sir Bedyvere carries his king to the water's edge. He softly lays him in the barge to be ferried away by the ladies in mourning. Below decks on the 'Victory' Nelson asks his friend, 'Kiss me, Hardy', worries about Lady Hamilton and his daughter, and dies whispering, 'God and my country'. Nelson enacts a scene repeated a thousand times before and since – behind ramparts, in trenches, on some bullet-swept no-man's-land, in jungle clearings. Cradled by the arms of weeping comrades, the hero dies in the hour of triumph.

Obvious and massive differences thwart any attempt to use such a death to gain insight into the crucifixion. If Nelson had survived the battle of Trafalgar totally unscathed, the victory would have been enhanced rather than diminished. His death added nothing to the triumph he had master-minded. But Good Friday could not have been the same, if Jesus had walked away unharmed. One gospel reports that the beloved disciple attended the crucifixion (John 19. 26f.). At the last supper he had lain 'close to the breast of Jesus' (John 13. 23), but on Calvary he remained a silent and helpless bystander. Jesus left his mother to the care of that friend, but did not ask him, 'Kiss me, John'. It would be depressingly silly to imagine the beloved disciple playing Hardy to a master who dies 'for God and Galilee'.

A few words of summary should be in order. Comparisons with heroes dying on battlefields – whether they be classical figures or contemporaries like Che Guevara and Camilo Torres – will hinder rather than help our insights into the crucifixion of Jesus. He resembled them in being a man committed to a cause who was slain by enemy soldiers. But no flow of words can erode the wall of differences – not least the fact that Jesus died a captive, whereas they remained in charge of their bodies till the end. As free agents they fell fighting in battle, whereas an army of occupation arrested Jesus and put him to death at its leisure.

Assassination

Victims of assassination seem to offer more promising perspectives for those seeking to 'place' the execution of Jesus. Mohandas Gandhi, John Kennedy, Martin Luther King and other such murdered leaders have impressed themselves on many contemporaries with the force of myth. Their violent deaths are among the handful of killings by which future generations will seek to know our century and give it a name. These assassinations have enjoyed a vivid and disturbing impact. It seems fair to add that they present some latter-day comparisons with the crucifixion on Calvary.

Gandhi and these others committed themselves to great human causes, became larger than life and drew lines across the surface of man's history. Even during their lifetime thousands – even millions – found courage and purpose by identifying with them. These leaders stood for persecuted people, oppressed nations and such new methods for securing justice as non-violent non-cooperation. Some, like King and Kennedy, resembled Jesus by dying young. Gandhi blended the austere asceticism of a John the Baptist with hints of Jesus' own gentler holiness. The Indian prophet was murdered as he climbed the steps of a prayer platform on his way to a regular prayer meeting. What we might call the 'geography' of death separates him from Jesus, who 'suffered outside the gate' (Heb. 13. 12) in a place which – from a cultic point of view – counted as totally profane. In the geography of their deaths Kennedy and King come closer to Jesus – the first being shot on a downtown street of Dallas and the other on the balcony of a Memphis motel. These everyday settings, while lacking the ugly associations of a hilltop appointed for public executions, resemble Calvary more than some holy place set aside for prayer.

All in all, such assassinated leaders and prophets can easily bring to mind Jesus' crucifixion. Innovative and dedicated men, they faced evil courageously, attracted the allegiance of millions, and aroused a hatred which eventually managed to do away with them.

Nevertheless, we need to count and bury the false implications in any effort to align even Gandhi's death too closely with Calvary. To begin with, these assassinated leaders had lived through years of busy activity before being murdered. Gandhi died at the age of seventy-eight, six months after his country finally won independence. Martin Luther King died at thirty-nine, but four-teen years of full-time ministry lay behind him. He had been the first American Negro to be named by *Time* magazine as 'Man of the Year', and the youngest person ever to receive the Nobel Peace Prize. The people of the United States made John Kennedy the first Catholic to occupy the White House. Years of work, obvious success and often the highest public recognition marked their lives. When they died by violence, the world drew its breath in horror and mourned their passing with epic splendour.

None of this applies to Jesus. At most his ministry lasted three years. Often he seemed like a man on the run, slipping away from murderous-minded enemies who gathered with stunning speed. No public prizes were thrust into his hand. Tiberius Caesar did not summon him to Rome and make him the first Jew to serve as consul, enjoy a triumph or receive some other massive mark of public honour. When he died on the cross, the world did not wince with pain. A handful of men and women scurried off into the dusk carrying his body to a secret burial.

Secondly, the unexpected nature of their deaths sets Gandhi and the other assassinated leaders apart from Jesus. To be sure, they could not presume that they were inviolate. Their principles put them in the firing line. Violent men had already threatened their lives. But no one could say for certain that a successful assassination attempt was to come – let alone know when this would happen. Death caught them unawares, flowed over them like lava and fixed them fast, before there could be any last suppers, final farewells, speeches from the scaffold or words from the cross. Abrupt assassination excluded the opportunity to take an active role by accepting the time, place and circumstances of their violent deaths.

In a sense the warriors slain in battle often had the edge here. They could foresee their death in some coming engagement. A last message gave meaning to their fate, and took away any impression of random bad luck. A little more than an hour before his ship came under fire, Nelson wrote in his private diary:

> May the Great God, whom I worship, grant to my Country, and for the benefit of Europe in general, a great and glorious victory; and may no misconduct in any one tarnish it; and may humanity after victory be the predominant feature in the British fleet. For myself, individually, I commit my life to Him who made me, and may His blessing light upon my endeavours for serving my Country faithfully. To Him I resign myself and the just cause which is entrusted to me to defend. Amen. Amen. Amen

Of course, this final entry bothers us today by its easy assumption, 'God is on my side'. But it puts a clear profile on Nelson's death, just as much as his celebrated signal before Trafalgar ('England expects that every man will do his duty') gave the force of myth to the victory itself. Most assassinated heroes, however, die 'untidy' deaths – robbed of any real chance to interpret and actively accept their end in the precise way it comes.

Finally, Kennedy and other victims of assassination attracted vast personality cults. Obsessive admiration flared up when they were murdered. But we may feel depressed to see how quickly these cults began to die with their departure from the scene. They had in fact only a precarious grip on mankind's imagination. No serious and sustained claim is made that they have somehow permanently saved the whole of humanity. These noble men are remembered with affection for having liberated some oppressed people and reconciled some alienated parties. They may even have given the world such a new theory and practice as Gandhi's non-violence. But the response to Jesus moved in its own growing and astonishing way.

His ante-mortem appeal, if considerable, remained limited to sections of the Palestinian population, and proved insufficient to save him from public execution. His post-mortem appeal has spread throughout the world. He is claimed to have liberated mankind from evil and reconciled it with God. This enduring response to Jesus' death separates him from any assassinated hero or – for that matter – from any other martyr.

The Martyrs

Martyrs form a coherent and distinctive group – from Socrates and the Maccabean martyrs through Ignatius of Antioch, Rabbi Akiba, Boethius, John Huss, Joan of Arc, Savonarola, Thomas More, Nicholas Ridley, Margaret Clitherow and Oliver Plunkett down to Charles Luanga and Dietrich Bonhoeffer. Violent death came in such a way that we can classify them with Jesus. Like him they not only refused to consider death as something to be shunned at all costs, but also they declined to remain passive victims. By maintaining their convictions and accepting their death, they transmuted it into a precious event, the end which gave point and purpose to their whole existence. Esteem for them endured and grew after death. They were like Jesus in that.

Particular circumstances also allow us to match the deaths of many martyrs with Jesus' own passion and crucifixion. Often betrayal by former friends or similar forms of treachery led to arrest and imprisonment. The unjust trials which preceded the death penalty frequently centred on some fatal question. Did Thomas More wish maliciously and traitorously to deprive Henry VIII of the title 'Supreme Head of the Church', which Parliament had granted him? How would Jesus answer when the high priest asked him 'Are you the Christ, the Son of the Blessed?' (Mark 14. 61). At times religious authorities joined state officials in staging these trials, bringing the accusations and reaching the required verdict of death. Thus Joan of Arc appeared before the court of the Bishop of Beauvais on charges of witchcraft and heresy. With depressing frequency the Christian church has been willing – through active involvement or default – to continue the role the Sanhedrin played in Jesus' execution.

Finally, many martyrs shared the same geography of death with Jesus – public execution. Some were, of course, butchered in their prison cells, or like Bonhoeffer led away to the sinister secrecy of a Nazi hanging. But Joan of Arc died in the Rouen market-place, Savonarola outside the Palazzo Vecchio, Ridley at a stake in the Broad and Plunkett at Tyburn. Sometimes we can compare the bystanders who came to the place of execution. Loyal to the last, several women watched Jesus die. When Thomas More was beheaded on Tower Hill, an adopted daughter (Margaret Clements) was the only member of his household who could endure to be present.

Granted some general similarities, we need to be sensitive to much that gives Jesus' passion and death its own particular profile. These differences go beyond the obvious and massive fact that no one even alleges that the other martyrs have reconciled the entire human race with God. More died for the unity of Christian Europe. He was never credited with giving his life to redeem the world. Such universal saving meaning has been attributed only to the martyrdom on Calvary. Besides this difference, however, there are other notable contrasts which we must not let slip out of sight. Groping greedily towards absolute power over his subjects, a vicious monarch struck down Thomas More. Days before his own suicide, a maniac dictator insisted on hanging Bonhoeffer – as part of a last struggle to exterminate his opponents. In the case of the crucifixion, however, it would be absurd to credit Pilate with the demonic stature of Henry VIII or Adolf Hitler.

Moreover, an ugly haste makes Jesus' execution different. Generally men took their time about killing martyrs. The Duke of Burgundy and then the English forces held Joan of Arc a prisoner for more than a year before burning her at the stake. Bonhoeffer's two years of imprisonment left him time to grow in faith, continue his journey of self-discovery and reach fresh insights that were to set post-war theological pulses racing. The rushed hours of his arrest, trial and execution gave Jesus no time to think through his identity and message – if we agree that such could have been a genuine possibility for him. He had no chance of learning lessons of patience, being taught by painful experiences and completing – so to speak – his moral and religious education.

Nor could Jesus do what many martyrs did in their cells – set down their faith in writing. Boethius' *Consolation of Philosophy*, More's *Dialogue of Comfort* and *Treatise on the Passion*, Ridley's farewell to Pembroke and Bonhoeffer's *Letters and Papers from Prison* gave shape and meaning to their death. From the cell of Pilate's praetorium Jesus left us no revised version of the Sermon on the Mount nor final edition of his parables. There was not even the opportunity to write some last instructions for his disciples or farewell message to his mother.

When we match martyrs, many of them split into two major groups: those who passionately prized death and those who sinfully recoiled from it. Jesus belonged to neither extreme. Ignatius of Antioch was a classic representative of the first group. As a prisoner being taken to Rome, he wrote to the Christians there and begged them not to prevent his martyrdom: 'You cannot do me a greater kindness than to allow me to be sacrificed unto God' (I. 2). 'I am willing', he explained, 'to die for God, unless you hinder me' (IV. 1). Ignatius longed to be torn and even wholly consumed by wild animals in a Roman arena.

> Suffer me to be food to the wild beasts, by whom I shall reach God. For I am the wheat of God; and I shall be ground by the teeth of the wild beasts, that I may be found the pure bread of Christ. Rather encourage the beasts, that they may become my sepulchre, and may leave nothing of my body; that being dead, I may not be troublesome to anybody; then I shall be truly the disciple of Jesus Christ (IV. 2).

He exploded with desire to face a fearful death and reach the company of Christ: 'Let fire and the cross; let the companies of wild beasts; let breakings of bones and tearing of members; let the shattering in pieces of the whole body, and all the wicked torments of the devil come upon me; only let me enjoy Jesus Christ' (V. 3). If Ignatius stood for one extreme, Thomas Cranmer represented those martyrs who weaved back and forth, hesitated, recanted, but finally found the iron in themselves and accepted death rather than betray their conscience. Jesus did not belong with those who desperately fended death off and sinfully ran away before bringing themselves finally to face their end. Nor did he belong, however, with those who hungered for death. On his last pilgrimage to Jerusalem he was no Ignatius writing letters ahead to dissuade friends from influencing the high priests and Pilate in his favour.

A further major contrast with many martyrs arises from what we might call the lack of style about Jesus' passion and death, when set against the martyrdom of men like Socrates and Thomas More. Plato's account of Socrates' trial and death arranges things so that there are no cracks in the walls of his master's performance. Socrates appears like the patron saint of all high-souled intellectual liberals misunderstood and finally destroyed by menacing, know-nothing illiberals. With tranquil detachment he accepts the verdict of the Athenian court, refuses the opportunity to escape, spends his last hours debating the immortality of the soul, drinks the hemlock, and dies with peace and poise. Plato's art successfully anaesthetizes us against feeling either real anger or profound pain at the unjust sentence and the brutal extinction of the old philosopher's life. Socrates himself never weeps over Athens. He does not have to express deep distress at any betrayal by friends. At the end he sends away his weeping wife and children. The disciples themselves stop weeping. The prison becomes transparent to eternal, universal realities, as Socrates speaks of the changeless world to which his soul will slip away without fear. Our attention shifts from the doomed man to that permanent, spiritual realm from which we come and to which we go. There are no ragged ends or rough edges in the martyrdom of Socrates.

Jesus, however, does not die with such style – particularly in the accounts offered by Mark and Matthew. In Gethsemane he suddenly becomes 'almost hysterical with terror and fear'. He hungers for comfort from his friends and an escape from death, but finds neither. Finally, he checks his panic, gets control over himself and accepts his destiny.[3] This struggle runs counter to the Platonic glorification of Socrates' calm and the English myth of the stiff upper lip. It prepares us to hear Jesus' tortured cry from the cross, 'My God, my God, why hast thou forsaken me?' (Mark 15. 34).

Let us take an example closer to our own times, the martyrdom of More. In his trial this former Lord Chancellor conducted himself with a skill and integrity that made him forever the darling of the English Bar. The case against More (that he had maliciously and traitorously rejected King Henry's title, Supreme Head of the Church) went badly, until Richard Rich gave evidence that More had uttered the fatal words in a conversation with him. In blazing terms More denied this evidence:

> If I were a man, my Lords, that did not regard an oath, I needed not, as it is well known, in this place, at this time, nor in this case, to stand here as an accused person. And if this oath of yours, Master Rich, be true, then pray I that I never see God in the face; which I would not say, were it otherwise, to win the whole world . . . In good faith, Master Rich, I am sorrier for your perjury than for my own peril.

It is hard to know whether to admire most either the martyr's lordly language and legal brilliance, or the gracious love and wit that flared up more than ever in his last days. Margaret Roper, his favourite daughter, rushed through the guard to embrace her father, when he was returning to the Tower of London after sentence of death had been passed. On the eve of execution he wrote to her:

> Tomorrow long I go to God: it were a day very meet and convenient for me. I never liked your manner toward me better than when you kissed me last: for I love when daughterly love and de ar charity hath no leisure to look to worldly courtesy. Farewell, my dear child, and pray for me, and I shall for you and all your friends, that we may merrily meet in Heaven.

More saw 'the humorous side of martyrdom'.[4] Clambering up the rickety steps to the scaffold, he asked: 'I pray you, Master Lieutenant, see me safe up, and for my coming down let me shift for myself.' Before he knelt for execution, he made a brief speech, protesting that he died 'the King's good servant but God's first'. R. W. Chambers calls these words 'the most weighty and the most haughty ever spoken on the scaffold. Dante could not have bettered them'.[5]

All of this is high drama, both stylish and moving, but none of it fits Jesus' death. In silence he listened to the false witnesses disagreeing among themselves. It is almost too painful to imagine his mother pushing through the Roman soldiers to embrace her son, or to think of him scribbling a final letter to her: 'Mother, I never liked your manner toward me better than when you kissed me last.' We would hideously trivialize the dragging agony of crucifixion to fancy that Christ could have said at Calvary, 'I pray you, Master Centurion, see me safe up the cross, and for my coming down let me shift for myself'. Perhaps Dante could hardly have bettered More's final words, but Jesus could not have uttered them. A death by torture killing did not allow for a brief but poised speech of farewell. There could be no humorous or haughty side to crucifixion.

Lastly, the disposal of his body detaches Jesus from other martyrs. The method chosen for killing them reduced Huss, Joan of Arc, Savonarola, Ridley and Bonhoeffer to ashes. Two other women helped Margaret Roper to bury her father's body, but the executioner placed the severed head on London Bridge. Jesus' body was neither dismembered nor destroyed by execution itself.

Apart from reporting that his side was pierced with a spear (John 19. 34), none of the gospels suggests that his body was violated after death. The chief priests mocked him when dying, but they shrank from mutilating his corpse once he was dead. Like Socrates he died without bones being broken or limbs removed. But then – unlike all other cases of martyrdom – the body of Jesus did not face the normal decomposition of the grave.

What has this chapter done for us? It could have made Jesus' execution impress itself on our imagination a little more sharply. To say that Jesus died by crucifixion may prove curiously empty, unless we can relate this killing to other classes of violent deaths. Of course, we do not really know in advance whether such comparisons will turn out important and enlightening for any of us. But reflection on other victims of man's passion to kill may build a context, in which we will appreciate more sharply the story of Good Friday. At any rate the classification and investigation of other violent deaths cannot substitute for a studious scrutiny of Jesus' own path to crucifixion. To this we turn in the next chapter.

II

JESUS ON THE RUN

Believe it, my brothers! He died too early; he himself would have recanted his teaching, had he lived to my age! He was noble enough to recant!

Nietzsche, *Thus Spoke Zarathustra*

The bitterest sorrow that man can know is to aspire to do much and to achieve nothing.

Herodotus, *History*

'What if' questions can sometimes throw light on the real course of events. What if Hitler had pulled back from invading Russia? What if Mao Tse-Tung had been killed during the long march? What if Cardinal Cajetan had lifted his head, smiled across the room and nodded agreement with Martin Luther? Such questions may flush out valuable insights about the self-destructive instinct of National Socialism, the fragile thread by which Chinese Communism survived, and the forces that hastened the bleeding and deepening religious revolts of the sixteenth century. 'What if' questions both express and arouse our wonder. What actually happened startles us. It could have been otherwise.

We trip up against some obvious 'what if' questions, as we move through the messy story of misunderstandings, brutality and chilling hatred that surrounded Jesus. What if the enraged members of the the Nazareth synagogue had succeeded in pitching him over the cliff on which their town stood (Luke 4. 28–30)?

What if Jesus had gone to Jerusalem with those Galileans 'whose blood Pilate mingled with their sacrifices', or been standing with the unlucky eighteen on whom an aqueduct tower collapsed (Luke 13. 1–4)? Or what if Jesus had failed to react quickly enough in the temple, when his enemies began prizing loose stones to hurl at him (John 8. 59)?

A Longer Life

We can, of course, speculate in the opposite direction, by imagining circumstances under which Jesus might have enjoyed a much *longer* life and died a natural death. His habit of solitary prayer could have taken over and driven him to a cave near the Dead Sea. There he might have dedicated his remaining years to contemplation, seeking his definitive role as a stable hermit and not as a wandering preacher. Or we could think of him anticipating Albert Schweitzer. What if Jesus had cut short his ministry of the word, found some Jericho road, and set himself up as a permanent Good Samaritan – caring for battered, hungry and homeless people? Or again Jesus could have waved goodbye to his disciples, walked back to Nazareth, married, raised a family, and let the veil of privacy slip down over the third stage of his life. He came from the grey obscurity of a Galilean village, and glowed with the fire of an urgent message. He could have gone home – a burnt-out revolutionary, content to live on quietly, get his prophetic challenge down in writing, and leave it to a startled world like some posthumous *Das Kapital*. Finally, it is fairly easy to imagine Jesus not only weeping over Jerusalem and denouncing the unbelieving cities of Galilee, but even throwing his hands up in despair over Palestine as a whole. Could he have slid off the scene to become an international missionary based on the imperial capital? After all he pointedly praised the Roman centurion whose servant he cured:

> Truly, I say to you, not even in Israel have I found such faith. I tell you, many will come from east and west and sit at table with Abraham, Isaac and Jacob in the kingdom of heaven, while the sons of the kingdom will be thrown into the outer darkness (Matt. 8. 10–12).

He noted how the scribes and Pharisees 'traversed land and sea to make a single proselyte' (Matt. 23. 15). Jesus could have left (or been ousted from) Palestine, made Rome his new headquarters, travelled incessantly, set up communities of disciples around the shores of the Mediterranean, and – let us imagine – disappeared on some last journey through northern Gaul.

What if Jesus had switched directions to become a desert father, a fulltime Good Samaritan, a married writer or a foreign missionary, and then died from some everyday disease or simple old age? He could have ticked off the years of a long life, his hair would have turned grey, he would have felt his fingers stiffen, he might have died cushioned lovingly by the arms of his children. Such hypotheses ought to please those who make much of the incarnation. They like to remind us insistently that by becoming man God entered fully into our human condition. The possibilities we have scanned show us Jesus grappling with things that make or break most men and women: failure in some major project, marriage, life abroad, sickness, the embarrassment of old age and the approach of natural death. He would no longer be floating free of much that fills and obsesses our thoughts. Besides, a change of course in his early thirties would link him to Ignatius Loyola, Martin Luther and similar religious leaders. They broke loose from previous commitments, lived on for decades, and shifted the course of world history by their mid-life decisions. 'Entering the human condition' should imply becoming open to such possibilities for religious development.

Nevertheless, these hypotheses about a longer life for Jesus most probably do not evoke a clamour of applause. It may be hard to put a finger on the cause of our unease. Perhaps it seems impossible to let the crucifixion go and still have our Christianity whole. Martyrdom stamps our image of Jesus. We cannot see what we might make of him, if he slipped out of life with a weeping family bending over his bed.

In a later chapter I want to discuss the 'weakness' of the crucified Jesus, which God made the 'place' of his liberating and reconciling power. Here let me say only this. Jesus could neither have been nor have seemed as totally and terribly 'weak', if he had turned into the greatest desert contemplative of all time, the first permanent Good Samaritan, a renowned but retired preacher who stunned the whole world with his posthumous masterpiece, or a first-century missionary who anticipated Billy Graham and outdistanced St Paul. In such cases we could only murmur our admiration at his success, not fall silent in horror at his fearful failure. We would be challenged by the power of his performance, not through the weakness of his pain.

An Earlier Death?

Let us go back to the violent deaths, which would have made Jesus' life even *shorter* than it turned out to be. His own townsfolk, Pilate's legionaries, a Jerusalem mob or some chance accident could have silenced Jesus months or more before the crucifixion was to come.

An ugly death by lynching almost followed Jesus' words in the Nazareth synagogue. If the infuriated congregation had succeeded, he would have died as the result of a prophetic challenge issued in a sacred place and during a religious function. Such a sudden death would have associated him with all those preachers murdered because of their sermons. His violent death would have enjoyed a similar religious setting, if he had been killed in the temple at Jerusalem. John reports that a menacing stoning-party gathered, when Jesus made a claim that has never ceased to startle: 'Truly, truly, I say to you, before Abraham was, I am' (John 8. 58). These were dangerous words to utter. At least once he undertook an equally risky action in the temple. He drove out those who profaned the sacred precincts by their business activities (Mark 11. 15–16). Jesus could not presume that the bankers, the traders and their bosses would treat him benevolently and shrink from striking back. It takes little effort to imagine them finishing him off then and there. In that case he would have died not only in a religious place, but also because he had acted as a religious man. His death would have come about precisely because he honoured the holiness of the temple, a building specially consecrated by the chosen people for their worship of God.

As it was, Jesus would not be slain in the temple nor after a synagogue ceremony. He died outside the proper place of religious people, away from the temple, all synagogues and other such sacred zones where men venerated God's special presence. He suffered a secular death which was profane to the point of extreme degradation. For he died as a condemned criminal by public execution in a place appointed for such executions. A more unholy death could scarcely be imagined than when Jesus 'suffered outside the gate' in a spot which – from a cultic point of view – counted as utterly profane. He once mentioned 'Zechariah, the son of Barachiah, murdered between the sanctuary and the altar' (Matt. 23. 35). But Jesus himself was not to die in such a holy setting like some first-century Thomas Becket. Neither Pilate nor Herod nor Caiaphas gave the necessary hint to their henchmen: 'Who will rid me of this turbulent preacher?' Christian piety long ago lost sight of the profane degradation which surrounded the crucifixion. Next to the Mamertine prison in Rome one can visit a *'sanctuary* of the *most holy* Crucified' (italics mine). In its barbaric reality Calvary was no sanctuary, but a harshly unholy place.

Death in a temple courtyard or at the bottom of the Nazareth cliff would have drastically altered the 'geography' of Jesus' death. Besides, the *timing* seems wrong. If mob violence abruptly flared up to destroy him, much of the dramatic power would drop out of the story. He would still be a *bona fide* martyr, if he were slain after a sermon, or for protesting against defilement of the temple, or for some admission about his true identity. But death would come too quickly for us to cope with it. In Luke's gospel Jesus arrives at Nazareth for a preaching engagement – fresh from his baptism and time in the desert. More than three chapters serve as overture, before Jesus begins his ministry with that first major sermon. It would seem grossly unfair, if the victim were not allowed to press ahead with his plans and bring them to some conclusion, successful or otherwise. One feels that he is entitled at least to try. A lynching right at the outset would rob him of that chance.

The gospel story respects our sense of timing, in that both 'sides' set themselves on collision course and keep to it. In Mark's gospel Pharisees and Herodians initiate joint plans to kill Jesus as early as chapter three, verse six. In John's version Jesus himself wastes little time before visiting Jerusalem, cleansing the temple and issuing his provocative statement about 'destroying' the temple (2. 13ff.). Nevertheless, both Jesus himself and those who line up against him do not rush at once to the climax. Tension must first mount. Once the arrest takes place in Gethsemane, he is driven at a savage pace to Calvary. Yet even the passion story wears an air of measured deliberateness. Men interrogate Jesus. He has time to respond. Unlike John, the other gospels, of course, place the cleansing of the temple shortly before the execution on Calvary. One could imagine a banker suddenly lunging forward with a dagger. It would not be surprising to find several sellers of animals abruptly clubbing Jesus to the ground. Or the whole crowd might surge over him in violent rage. But this death scene at the close of the ministry would occur with the absurd speed of a flash flood. Even at the end such a temple lynching could not satisfactorily replace the passion story, as we have it. In three of the four gospels a crowd will gather for Jesus' trial before Pilate. But they do not plunge forward in rage to kill Jesus with irrational haste. The story pushes ahead steadily to a death some hours later in the day.

Luke's reference to the eighteen victims crushed by a collapsing building allows us to raise 'what if' questions about such everyday accidents. What if Jesus' corpse were among those to be dug out from the rubble, after the tower of Siloam suddenly buckled and fell? What if a runaway Roman chariot had knocked him down as he crossed the main street of Capernaum? Would it have made any difference, if he had drowned in a boating accident, caught a fatal attack of pneumonia after a night out in the Galilee hills, or died in some other unexpected but 'natural' way during the course of his ministry? Such deaths belong to our everyday world. They match neatly the incarnational principle given its classical form by Kierkegaard: 'If the contemporary generation [of Jesus] had left nothing behind them but these words: "We have believed that in such and such a year the God appeared among us in the humble figure of a servant, that he lived and taught in our community, and finally died," it would be more than enough.'[1]

The appearance and humble life of the God-man satisfies Kierkegaard. The manner of Jesus' death remains unspecified and – seemingly – unimportant. A bolting horse, a careless engineer, a common virus or a snap storm could cut his life short. But in that case it would look quaint to claim that such a death liberated mankind from the power of evil and reconciled us all with God. We would be saved through a piece of bad luck! Such accidents could happen to any of us, regardless of our status and commitments. Only a brave or foolish man, of course, would assert that God *could* never choose such a method for the world's salvation. What we dismiss as bad luck God might see as a peculiarly appropriate way for freeing and reconciling the human race. Nevertheless, we could only shake our heads in puzzlement over the divine choice. If some adjustments to Cleopatra's nose might have diverted the course of human history, so a less fractious horse, a more careful engineer, a less vigorous virus or a less violent storm could have blocked or at least delayed the central event in man's salvation. Such a notion can only seem odd. We could hardly respond to a death brought by bad luck, as we respond to the crucifixion. Any 'Cleopatra's nose' view of redemption leaves us dissatisfied.

Similar difficulties arise over possibilities involving the Roman army of occupation. What if Jesus had been one of a hundred hostages killed in reprisal for a successful night operation carried out by Zealot guerrillas? It takes no great effort to imagine Jesus rounded up at random and driven to his death in some first-century Ardeatine caves. That would make him the chance victim of a Roman atrocity, another casualty in the history of ruthless over-reaction.

During his ten years as governor of Judaea (AD 26–36), Pilate in particular showed that he could be both edgy and brutal when he faced or even suspected trouble. Eventually an episode in Samaria resulted in his being withdrawn from command and summoned to face charges in Rome. A large group of Samaritans had gathered at the foot of Mount Gerizim, after it was rumoured that some sacred vessels hidden by Moses had been unearthed. Pilate sent in his cavalry and foot soldiers. Some Samaritans were killed in the fighting which broke out. Others were captured and then executed on the governor's orders.[2]

Pilate could readily have feared political and even military challenges from the people who streamed from all over Palestine to hear Jesus preach. John's gospel notes that one crowd tried to seize Jesus and proclaim him king (6. 15). What if Pilate had secretly arranged with the ruler of Galilee, Herod Antipas, to send in the troops? The Sermon on the Mount could have ended in shrieks and screams, as Roman cavalry thudded up the slopes. What if Jesus had died then – the victim of a Roman governor's mistake? He would be just another casualty in a misguided military operation, just another victim of an army of occupation intent on terrorizing the civilian population into submission. We could hardly call such a death martyrdom in the full sense. Jesus would belong with the victims of those chilling massacres in Amritsar, Armenia, Drogheda, Sharpeville, towns all over Eastern Europe and ever so many other bloodstained places in our world.

But perhaps we have seen enough of these 'what if' questions. If any of them enables us to get a sharper focus on Jesus' actual death, well and good. There seems little point in pushing on further to wild questions like 'what if Martians had killed him?' Nevertheless, before we break loose from the matter, it is worth glancing back over the centuries to the third part of Aquinas'

Summa Theologica. Without obsessively grinding away at such questions, St Thomas speculates about the time, place and manner of Jesus' end: Could he have died after a longer life, or been killed in the temple, or been burnt to death (qu.46, a.4,9,10)? Our 'what if' questions enjoy an impeccable ancestry in the Middle Ages. But it is high time to examine the gospel story as we have it. Let us consider how Jesus himself and those around him moved towards the crucifixion. This can offer us a way in.

The Opponents Gather

The opposition to Jesus gathered with savage speed. By the end of his brief ministry almost everyone seemed to have turned on him or left him. Hostility and misunderstanding began at home. 'His family' set out 'to take charge of him; for people were saying that he was out of his mind' (Mark 3. 21).[3] It was little wonder that his immediate relatives failed to sympathize and side with him. His message cut across natural and traditional family ties. He expected that his close followers would be ready to imitate the kind of break he had already made himself: 'There is no one who has left house or brothers or sisters or mother or father or children or lands, for my sake and for the gospel, who will not receive a hundredfold in this time . . . and in the age to come eternal life' (Mark 10. 29f.). Jesus' mother and brothers had to listen to him proclaiming to the world that he put his new brotherhood and sisterhood above any claims based just on blood relationship (Mark 3. 31–35). After this early passage in Mark's narrative we never hear again of his mother and his brothers. They simply drop out of sight for good. According to John's gospel, his brothers press Jesus to court publicity at the feast of tabernacles (7. 2–10). They then disappear from the story. We pick up one further reference to his family. Twelve chapters later his mother joins her sister (Mary the wife of Cleopas), Mary Magdalene and the beloved disciple at the foot of the cross. Two or three relatives remain anchored to Jesus right to the end.[4] The others leave him to the brutal fate that his 'mad' way of acting has invited.

The village people, with whom Jesus lived as child, boy and man, gave him up long before the crucifixion. As we have seen Luke tells how they tried to lynch him after one synagogue service. In Mark's account they shook their dull heads in puzzlement over what Jesus was up to – trotting out pieces of wise teaching and even showing that he might be a bit of a miracle-worker (6. 1–2). But they knew who he was and could cut him down to size: 'Is not this the carpenter, the son of Mary and brother of James and Joses and Judas and Simon, and are not his sisters here with us?' (6.3). The Nazarenes fell foul of Jesus. Perhaps they had never liked him anyway.

Galilee as a whole finally disappointed Jesus. He lashed out at the towns which stuck safely to their sins – despite all his miracles:

> Woe to you, Chorazin! Woe to you, Bethsaida! For if the mighty works done in you had been done in Tyre and Sidon, they would have repented long ago in sackcloth and ashes. But I tell you, it shall be more tolerable on the day of judgment for Tyre and Sidon than for you. And you, Capernaum, will you be exalted to heaven? You shall be brought down to Hades . . . it shall be more tolerable on the day of judgment for the land of Sodom than for you (Matt. 11. 21–24).

Unlike John the Baptist (Mark 6. 20), Jesus never had – nor apparently ever sought – the chance of converting Galilee's ruler, Herod Antipas. When warned of threats from that quarter, Jesus refused to let himself be hustled:

> Some Pharisees came, and said to him, 'Get away from here, for Herod wants to kill you.' And he said to them, 'Go and tell that fox, "Behold I cast out demons and perform cures today and tomorrow, and the third day I finish my course. Nevertheless I must go on my way today and tomorrow and the day following; for it cannot be that a prophet should perish away from Jerusalem" ' (Luke 13. 31–33).

Nevertheless, Herod would hardly have scrupled to do away with the cousin of the prophet he had already murdered. Galilee endangered Jesus, as well as disappointing him.

During his ministry opposition to Jesus sprang from the Pharisees. Doubtless the gospels tend to exaggerate in putting these critics in an ugly light, but there seems no effective reason for doubting the substantial reality of their attacks. It could well have looked as if Jesus' stress on inner motivation would result in people failing to observe the law externally. Besides he maintained vigorously a hierarchy of values in his moral thinking. For him the value of restoring a human being to health bulked larger than the regular prohibition of work on the sabbath (Mark 3. 1–5). Unspoken fears and open disagreement appear to have led some Pharisees to a steady hostility towards Jesus. The grinding taxes that had to be paid to the Roman Emperor allowed them to lay a trap. To their astonishment he slipped past the dilemma they posed without making any blatantly pro-Roman or anti-Roman statement: 'Render to Caesar the things that are Caesar's, and to God the things that are God's'(Mark 12. 17).

The chief priests and other Sadduccees also lined up against Jesus. Toward the close of the ministry it had become clear that no major religious and/or political group in Galilee and Judea would defend him. Some support from ordinary pilgrims flared up when he entered Jerusalem (Mark 11. 1–10). But it faded quickly enough for the chief priests to plan their arrest. He celebrated the Last Supper for a disintegrating community. Judas led the temple police to seize Jesus, the other disciples rushed away, and a few hours later Peter denied on oath that he had ever known his master. With the collapse of Jesus' new brotherhood, all support has vanished.

The world which Jesus challenges to repent and turn back to God's love rapidly turns dangerous. He stands on the shoulders of John the Baptist to make a vivid impact at the start. But then some simply quit his cause. Others threaten him. He quickly becomes a man on the run. At times he appears stunned, wondering what he has unleashed or why he has failed: 'O Jerusalem, Jerusalem, killing the prophets and stoning those who are sent to you! How often would I have gathered your children together as a hen gathers her brood under her wings, and you would not!' (Luke 13. 34). Even before the final arrest takes place, it looks as if he is only alive by accident. Not that there is *one* implacable and unpleasant foe, who hounds Jesus relentlessly and finally hunts him down after several narrow escapes. Neither Herod nor Caiaphas nor Pilate plays the part of the pitiless pursuer. But death itself stands behind the whole story. According to Luke, the ministry opens with an attempted lynching at Nazareth. Early on in his narrative Mark notes that the Pharisees put their heads together with the Herodians to fix a plan for killing Jesus (3. 6). Matthew sets the outbreak of the murderous violence right back in Jesus' infancy. Joseph has hardly bundled Mary and the baby out of Bethlehem, before Herod the Great swoops to massacre all the male infants in the area. The world of the gospels does not wait till the end before getting its knives out. Long before then it has begun its killings. It claims unnatural victims in the young children slain in Bethlehem. John the Baptist looks more like a natural victim. After all he invites trouble by walking into the presence of Herod Antipas to rebuke the king: 'It is not lawful for you to have your brother's wife.' But the manner of the prophet's death is disgusting. His freshly severed head is carried down the royal banqueting hall like another dish of food (Mark 6. 17–29). Are the guests so far gone with drink and lust that they hardly notice, and even this obscene murder cannot disturb the party?

Towards Calvary

In moving towards his crucifixion Jesus never seems to presume that the world will treat him benevolently, or that unlike his cousin John and other martyred prophets he is somehow inviolate. At times he has to take quick self-preservative action, if he is to escape being killed. But death does not eventually strike him down, because he gets careless and ceases to do anything really effective in his own defence. We are not faced with a failure of will and imagination. Jesus is no weary hero in a Western, no soldier suffering from combat fatigue. Nor does the end come, because he turns to make a stand – realizing that he cannot run without having to run forever. There are no villains in pursuit, with whom Jesus decides to face his high noon in Jerusalem.

Piet Schoonenberg points us in the right direction here. He suggests that Jesus has to shift from identifying his role as preaching the good news of God's kingdom.

> Only when the opposition grows and these opponents develop a truly deadly hatred of him, there dawns upon him the significance of the violent death which awaits him. Now he recognizes from the circumstances that his Father's will for him is to fulfil the function of the Servant of Yahweh to the end, to die in order to bring the many to righteousness. Thus his horizon broadens out from the lost sheep of Israel to Jew and gentile, and his mission develops from that of a prophet proclaiming salvation to that of the victim bringing salvation.[5]

There are things here that we may want to challenge. But the notion of a shift in perspective provides the correct clue to the story.

Jesus does not leave Nazareth to be baptized by John and begin his mission like a Kamikaze pilot. As soon as he climbs into the cockpit, the pilot has passed the point of no return. But Jesus' course of action, once embarked upon, fails to come across as immediately and really irreversible. It takes some time to reach the point of no return, when he can no longer go home again to Nazareth if he so chooses. His ministry is not some self-destructive, Kamikaze-style rush to Calvary. At least the first three gospels fail to tell the story that way. Jesus does not know from the outset that something dreadful waits for him at the end of the road – let alone deliberately aim at dying violently by crucifixion.

Initially he dedicates all his energy to a task where success can be measured in human terms – the religious revival of Israel. He picks up where his cousin left off: 'The time is fulfilled, and the kingdom of God is at hand; repent, and believe in the gospel' (Mark 1. 15). Jesus begins to talk of human obedience towards God with a deep moral earnestness. He knows as well as anyone that death will submerge every earthly task or interest – sacred or secular. But without a trace of morbid contempt he faces the whole of life, and disdains nothing for being transient. The full span of human experience matters to him: a farmer trudging up and down as he sows his crop, sparrows seen fluttering dead to the ground, a boy who takes his money and runs away from home, a poor widow making her small contribution to the temple funds, kings planning a military campaign, business men unable to repay loans. Jesus neither despises nor discards any person or any activity, and brings his good news to bear upon it. He assures his audience that nothing of our human reality lacks worth and value in the sight of God: 'The very hairs on your head are numbered!' (Luke 12. 7).

He never urges his hearers to detach themselves from the worthless things of the body, or to seek release from the ills of earthly existence. In fact his miracles aim at restoring people to complete bodily integrity. Those who are cured can now see, walk erect, cook meals, and live again with their families in a normal human fashion. Sickness has cut them off from the full range of physical activity. In the case of lepers their disease has excluded them from living in cities or villages with other men and women. By healing the sick Jesus reinserts them into human society. His miraculous deeds result in a wholesome rehumanizing. He enables the sick or the handicapped to enjoy once again complete bodily welfare as ordinary men and women.

All of this contrasts sharply with the attitude of Socrates, as it is lovingly described in the *Phaedo*. He sees true life as entailing nothing less than a strict preparation for death. The philosopher rehearses dying, longs to escape from imprisonment by the body, and welcomes death as the gateway to the real, spiritual world. As he waits for the gaoler to bring the hemlock, Socrates explains to his friends why 'a man who has really spent his life in philosophy is naturally glad when he is on the point of dying':

Those who apply themselves correctly to the pursuit of philosophy are in fact practising nothing more nor less than dying and death. If this is so, it would indeed be strange that men who had throughout their lives sought precisely this, should grumble when it came – the very thing which they had, for so long, desired and rehearsed.[6]

Jesus, however, teaches people to practise living, not to rehearse dying. Even if the evangelist himself creates the actual words, the Fourth Gospel catches nicely the thrust of Jesus' ministry: 'I came that they may have life, and have it more abundantly' (10. 10). Jesus could never say: 'I came that they may practise death, and rehearse it more professionally.' When he himself reaches 'the point of dying', he cries out against it rather than showing himself 'naturally glad'. He never urges his audience: 'Emancipate yourselves from the bondage of flesh by discipline, detachment and prayer. The life of the Spirit after death is the only reality.'

The preaching of Jesus neither morbidly dwells on the thought of death nor avoids the topic altogether. One parable describes the foolish farmer who plans to build new granaries. He wants to enjoy himself for years on the proceeds of a bumper harvest, but he dies without warning (Luke 12. 16–21). The story about the rich man and Lazarus punches a warning at us about the need to repent before the end (Luke 16. 19–31). Yet we would misrepresent Jesus' ministry, if we summed it all up as a cry, 'Prepare for death!'. Rather in his own unique way he pushes at people the message: 'Practise true life!'. He is no Platonist anxious to shed the body, set the soul free and get away to the real world. Still less is the first-century existentialist insisting that suicide is the only genuine question. He never gives grounds that might encourage anyone to opt for self-extinction over life. Nor could Jesus accept the moral that Sigmund Freud drew from *King Lear* – that we should 'renounce life and renounce love and make friends with the necessity of dying'.

Christian asceticism has itself included a hardy tradition which represents life as a persistent *preparatio mortis*. The *Imitation of Christ* warns us: 'Thou ought so to order thyself in all thy thoughts and actions, as if today thou wert to die' (I. 23). We hear similar advice fron Angelus Silesius: 'Think upon death, Christian: why think of the rest? There is nothing more profitable one can think upon than the manner in which we should die.'[7] Now set the Sermon on the Mount (Matt. 5–7) alongside these two warnings. Jesus yields to no one in his ultimate seriousness. But – rather than calling for the constant contemplation of death – he invites us to seek 'God's kingdom and his righteousness', refrain from being 'anxious about tomorrow', and realize that today has enough troubles of its own (6. 33f.). Jesus wants us to 'think upon' *his words* and to put them into practice – not to brood endlessly upon death. He is too busy speaking of life to lapse into any sombre obsession with mortality. The Sermon on the Mount gathers up a generous armful of human experiences: the sight of a hilltop town, quarrels between brothers, the administration of the law, men lusting after other men's wives, houses ransacked by thieves, buildings demolished by flood. But Jesus never bothers to evoke that common experience which the *Imitation of Christ* recalls: 'If at any time thou hast seen another man die, make account that thou must also pass the same way' (I. 23). To put this in an extreme way. We never hear Jesus asking: 'Have you seen a man die? Keep recalling that you must pass the same way. Truly, I say to you, I have seen men crucified, and I keep recalling that I must also pass the same way.' Jesus does not anticipate later Christian tradition by urging the duty to contemplate death and prepare for it.

Eventually, of course, Jesus does start to speak of his coming death. Let me set out the three passion predictions which punctuate Mark's narrative:

> The Son of man must suffer many things, and be rejected by the elders and the chief priests and the scribes, and be killed, and after three days rise again (8. 31).

> The Son of man will be delivered into the hands of men, and they will kill him; and when he is killed, after three days he will rise (9. 31).

> The Son of man will be delivered to the chief priests and the scribes, and they will condemn him to death, and deliver him to the Gentiles; and they will mock him, and spit upon him, and scourge him, and kill him; and after three days he will rise (10. 33–34).

It is worth reminding ourselves that these passages occur only after Mark has told the first part of the story. Up the end of chapter eight life-talk dominates. In the first half of the gospel Jesus has practically nothing to say about death. He refers vaguely to the time when the bridegroom will be taken away from the wedding guests (2. 20), and before curing a man with a withered hand he asks bluntly: 'Is it lawful on the sabbath to do good or to do harm, to save life or to kill?' (3. 4). In the narrative we hear of a plot against his life (3. 6), the mass suicide of some

Gerasene swine (5. 13), and John's martyrdom (6. 17–29). We learn that the little daughter of Jairus dies – only to be restored to life by Jesus (5. 22–24, 35–43). During the first half of Mark's gospel Jesus drives out demons, heals the sick, feeds the hungry, and proclaims that God's kingdom is growing with mysterious power like the life of nature itself (4. 26f.). He is too busy communicating life to speak of death.

From chapter eight, verse thirty-one the perspective changes. The miracles dwindle away. The crowds thin out, and mostly Jesus remains alone with his core group of disciples. He explains that 'the Son of man came . . . to give his life as a ransom for many' (10. 45). He tells a parable in which the tenants of a vineyard do not scruple to murder even the owner's son (12. 1–11). He warns of Jerusalem's destruction and the world's end (13. 1–37), when 'brother will deliver up brother to death, and the father his child, and children will rise against parents and have them put to death' (13. 12). He defends the woman who pours a jar of expensive ointment over his head: 'She has done what she could; she has anointed my head beforehand for burial' (14. 8). The story presses on quickly to the Last Supper, where Jesus takes a cup of wine and passes it to the twelve with the words, 'This is my blood of the covenant, which is poured out for many'(14. 24). The agony in Gethsemane and his arrest follow at once.

In Mark's story the switch of perspective comes fairly abruptly. Men have initiated plots against Jesus' life. Then he himself blurts out the news to his dismayed disciples that a violent death awaits him. Unlike Mark, Luke introduces this announcement well short of the half-way mark in his gospel (9. 22). The Fourth Gospel goes even further. John the Baptist introduces Jesus as the sacrificial 'Lamb of God, who takes away the sin of the world' (1. 29). Right from the start Jesus appears aware of his 'hour' – the passion, death and resurrection towards which he moves with inexorable dignity (2. 4; 7. 6, 30; 8. 20). By flatly claiming power over his own life, the Johannine Jesus can make us uneasy.[8] What confronts us here but suicide? Doesn't this human life become cruelly incredible, being lived under a conscious countdown to death by torture killing? What sense can we make of one who anticipates and accepts from the outset a predetermined crucifixion? However, we need to offset this impression by noting at least three things. Jesus implies no precise date by 'my hour', as if he could at any moment state just how many months and days of life he had left. This 'hour' includes his resurrection and glorification.

We misrepresent matters grossly, if we think simply of an execution. Finally, the Fourth Gospel admittedly allows for no change of perspective. The Johannine Jesus is always moving towards his 'hour'. Nevertheless, this gospel never includes in its advance warning of the passion the kind of grim details about scourging, mockery and other sufferings which Mark inserts in his passion predictions. To be sure, the text hints at crucifixion when Jesus speaks of his being 'lifted up' (3. 14; 8. 28; 12. 32f.).[9] But nothing like Mark's third prediction (10. 33–34) surfaces in the Fourth Gospel. This gospel not only leaves the external picture of the passion vague when it announces Jesus' coming end, but (unlike Mark) also introduces a rich theological content into those announcements. The 'lifting up' will 'draw all men' to him – the saving antitype of the brazen serpent which Moses raised before the Israelites to deliver them. Both the presence of such theological interpretation and the absence of historical detail help to mitigate the sense that John's gospel portrays a conscious countdown to murder.

To come back to Mark, which the authors of Matthew and Luke use in writing their gospels. One might admit that the story of these three gospels *considered as story* represents – or at least suggests – that Jesus' perspective shifts from being a prophet proclaiming salvation to being the victim whose death brings salvation. But can we peer through the story and find that *the historical Jesus actually did shift* from engaging himself with preaching the coming kingdom to accepting a victim-role? This is not to demand that we necessarily identify the time at which such a change took place. But are there real reasons for concluding that such a shift did occur at some point during his ministry?

Two lines of argument converge to argue for a change of perspective on the part of the historical Jesus. First of all, he at least *began* by following John the Baptist and calling for repentant belief in the face of God's coming rule. To be sure, Jesus stood apart from his precursor in important ways. Divine judgment seems to have bulked larger in John's call for conversion. Jesus preached a joyful message by representing in his own person God's message of mercy towards sinners who were willing to repent. John worked no miracles, while Jesus appears to have healed the sick and practised exorcisms from an early stage in his ministry, if not right from the outset. Granted these and further differences, Jesus at any rate echoed something of John's message by announcing that 'the kingdom of God is at hand; repent, and believe in the gospel'. He did not begin by proclaiming that 'my crucifixion is at hand; repent, and believe in the kingdom of God which will come with my death'. When Jesus, however, eventually celebrated the Last Supper with his core group of disciples, he spoke of his blood which was to be 'poured out for many', his life given for all (Mark 14. 24). Of course, one must ask here: How far has the eucharistic celebration of the early Christians shaped the narrative which Mark incorporates? Nevertheless, at the very least one saying goes back to Jesus himself and can hardly derive from the later liturgy of the church: 'Truly, I say to you, I shall not drink again of the fruit of the vine until that day when I drink it new in the kingdom of God' (14. 25). Here he linked his impending death with the coming rule of God. Somewhere along the line since his baptism by John and the opening of his ministry, Jesus began to talk and – presumably – to think in a different way about the relationship between the kingdom and his own vocation.

Secondly, a shift in perspective also emerges from an examination of Q. This common collection of sayings on which Matthew and Luke drew contains nothing at all about Jesus' death. We simply look in vain for material on that topic. Q includes warnings that the disciples must reckon on being rejected and persecuted (Luke 6. 22 = Matt. 5. 11). The closest one comes to any hint of Jesus' own destiny comes in a saying about the violent fate of prophets:

> Therefore also the Wisdom of God said, 'I will send them prophets and apostles, some of whom they will kill and persecute', that the blood of all the prophets, shed from the foundation of the world, may be required of this generation, from the blood of Abel to the blood of Zechariah, who perished between the altar and the sanctuary. Yes, I tell you, it shall be required of this generation (Luke 11. 49–51 = Matt. 23. 34–36).

Even if we sense overtones about Jesus' own violent death, the logion fails to allude clearly to the crucifixion. The argument from Q is this. No scholar denies that at least some sayings represented by Q derive from Jesus himself. Q gives us a measure of insight into what was actually said during the course of the ministry. The man whose preaching included those logia does not sound like one who anticipates and accepts the role of a martyrdom which brings salvation to others. There is a shift from the preacher of Q to the suffering Jesus of the passion story.

One could always suppose a gap between the preacher's words

and the preacher's thoughts. Could we maintain that from the outset Jesus understood that he was to bring salvation through his violent death? He carried this 'suffering secret' around with him, but only broke the news about it shortly before his passion. Obviously one cannot rule out absolutely this 'suffering secret' hypothesis. In theory, Jesus the preacher could have kept his grim secret to himself. But no evidence like a private diary or any confidential letters to a close friend survives to support such an hypothesis.

If we agree that the historical Jesus did shift from engagement with his ministry to accept a victim-role, we can seek reasons for this shift. Meditation on the vocation of God's suffering servant might have prompted the insight and its acceptance. Reflection on the fate of prophets in general and on John the Baptist in particular could also have encouraged Jesus' change of perspective. However, a prophetic vocation did not always involve violent death. John's own martyrdom did not quite match the path to death Jesus took. Let me explain. Quoting an unknown source, Jesus remarked that 'the Wisdom of God said, "I will send them prophets and apostles, some of whom they will kill and persecute" ' (Luke 11. 49). In Matthew's version some of these divine servants suffer persecution but not violent death: 'I send you prophets and wise men and scribes, some of whom you will kill and crucify, and some you will scourge in your synagogues and persecute from town to town' (23. 34). But in the passion predictions attributed to him, Jesus spoke unhesitatingly of death and did not stop softly at some less terrible news: 'The Son of man will continue to meet opposition and may be killed. If that happens, after three days he must rise again.' If Jesus had the fate of prophets in mind, he aligned himself above all with those who died violently.

The specific fate of John the Baptist obviously hung over Jesus' ministry. John deliberately courted danger by stalking into Herod's presence to confront that petty tyrant over his irregular marriage situation. Earlier the Baptist had lashed many Pharisees and Sadducees (Matt. 3. 7–10), but they took no part in his murder. When he made his move from the Jordan, he picked on Herod! Antigone risked death by defying a ruler and burying her brother – an act required both by natural piety and Greek religion. But the gospels do not claim that either his prophetic vocation or some special divine revelation *obliged* John to make his challenge. Did he yearn to prove himself in one supreme test? At any rate his prophetic *word* of denunciation led to a death far from Jerusalem, the heart of Jewish religious life. According to Josephus, John died in the fortress of Machaerus on the east side of the Dead Sea.[10] We can echo and adapt Hebrews to say that John 'suffered outside the people'. Jesus' prophetic *action* in cleansing the temple undoubtedly helped to bring about his execution, but the crucifixion took place only 'outside the gate'. In any case, he never followed his cousin's example by seeking out, rebuking and provoking Herod, Pilate, Caiaphas or some other powerful individual. John the Baptist's fate may not have shaped Jesus' thinking and acting nearly as much as is often supposed. Jesus ignored John – or at least the geography of his martyrdom – in making the sweeping generalization, 'It cannot be that a prophet should perish away from Jerusalem' (Luke 13. 33).

Whatever the precise historical background, the cross begins to cast its shadow over Mark's story from the end of chapter eight. Curiously, however, the manner of Jesus' violent death remains unspecified until the crowd cries out, 'Crucify him!' (15. 13). The passion predictions content themselves with speaking in general of his being 'killed'. At any rate from the half-way mark, death-talk glides into Mark's narrative. Jesus has lived intensely – healing broken lives and bodies, and producing a vivid and disturbing impact on his audiences. We now learn that he is not going to get out of it alive. The pallor of death begins to enfold him. No talk of love relieves the deadly chill of these passion predictions. They fail to explain that 'love will deliver the Son of man into the hands of men'. Even the most cheerful exegesis cannot exorcize the frightening, impersonal ring about the words, 'The Son of man *must* suffer many things and be killed.'

On the eve of execution how did Jesus envisage and face his end? Put just like that, the question can make us uneasy and evasive. How can we really know what went through his mind as the crucifixion closed in? The early Christians who handed on the passion story and the evangelists who wrote it all up lacked our psychological curiosity. They hardly ever mentioned Jesus' motivation. In general what they left us makes it notoriously difficult to penetrate his inner life. As stories, the gospels look to the public side of things. They seem to afford neither data nor encouragement for reflecting psychologically on his experience. Even if they had given us more than just the agony in Gethsemane and a few other hints, we might disown the effort on grounds of doctrine or reverence. Are we either competent or genuinely good enough to judge the quality of his mind? This case against investigating Jesus' attitude towards his end is familiar and forceful. Yet nothing is to be gained by refusing at least to put the question, reflecting on other martyrs and exploiting the possibilities that Mark's text offers us.

We can begin by quietly striking out certain states of mind suggested by martyrs like Socrates, Joan of Arc, Thomas More, Thomas Cranmer and Dietrich Bonhoeffer. Jesus does not regard his impending death as the God-given chance to expiate *his own* sins of omission or commission. The sentiments of Dag Hammarskjöld fail to fit Jesus at the Last Supper or in Gethsemane:

> To-morrow we shall meet,
> Death and I –
> And he shall thrust his sword
> Into one who is wide awake.
>
> But in the meantime how grievous the memory
> Of hours frittered away.[11]

Whatever Jesus did before his baptism by John, he never gives the slightest sign of recalling sadly those 'hours frittered away'. Cranmer's martyrdom stands even further away from the crucifixion. After repeatedly changing his beliefs and writing recantations, he finally realizes that he must cling to certain positions – no matter what Queen Mary and the Parliament might order him to believe. He renounces the 'things written with his hand, contrary to the truth which he thought in his heart'. As the fire rises around him, he says, 'This hand hath offended', and holds it firmly in the flames until it is consumed. It would be bitterly absurd to imagine Jesus deciding at the end that he sinned by working miracles on the sabbath, and stretching out his hands for the nails with the admission, 'These hands have offended'. He prays right to the end – but never for forgiveness.

Can we entertain hypotheses that propose, not repentance for sins, but growth in self-knowledge? During his imprisonment Bonhoeffer revises his interpretations of himself and his work. He begins to recognize consciously what he perhaps 'really' knew all the time, but has been unable to formulate. In the Letter to the Hebrews one passage appears to echo Jesus' Gethsemane experience:

> In the days of his flesh, Jesus offered up prayers and supplications,
> with loud cries and tears, to him who was able to save him from death,

and he was heard for his godly fear. Although he was a Son, he learned obedience through what he suffered (5. 7–8).

Can we press this line further and view the passion as initiating or at least completing a process of growth? Is death the price Jesus must pay, if he is to cease thinking in exactly the same terms as he did when John baptized him, and finally see his life for what it is? In that case Jesus would undergo an accelerated version of Bonhoeffer's experience. Nothing in Mark's narrative, however, suggests giving an affirmative answer here. In the few hours of his passion Jesus does not make any crowning discovery about himself and the meaning of life. His moral education is not suddenly completed. The *psychological* truth which Hebrews may easily suggest to us – that people may learn from their sufferings – suits Jesus' previous failure rather than his final hours. Let us come back to that point shortly. Hebrews gets close to a *theological* principle which will be taken up in a later chapter – 'the uncrucified is the unhealed'.

The martyrdoms of Socrates, Joan of Arc and Thomas More also fail to yield precise patterns for interpreting Jesus' state of mind on the eve of crucifixion. Socrates believes his sentence to be unjust, but he respects the Athenian laws so much, that he will not violate them by escaping from prison and slipping away into exile. Jesus, however, does not accept death out of some desire to uphold the rule of Jewish or Roman law. Nor does he court execution because he sticks doggedly to some very specific claim – that he has, let us say, heard the divine voice in the desert. Loyalty to her voices leads Joan to the stake. The pressures on Jesus do not threaten his integrity in quite that way. The motivation behind More's martyrdom also leaves us with some sharp contrasts. On the one hand, More dies for the unity of Christendom – 'in and for the Faith of the Holy Catholic Church', as he says on the scaffold. He has not provoked Henry VIII's schism, but like John Fisher, some Carthusians and others he refuses to accept it. On the other hand, up to the time of his condemnation he maintains that liberty of conscience gives him the legal right to remain silent about the new title given by Parliament to the king. More does not seek death by speaking against Henry's claim to be 'Supreme Head of the Church'. When martyrdom looms up, he shows himself grateful for the honour being bestowed upon him. None of this fits Jesus. He does not die for the unity of the Jewish faith throughout the Mediterranean world. Rather, he refuses to give up trying to reform Israel even at the price of schism: 'Do you think that I have come to give peace on earth? No, I tell you, but rather division; for henceforth in one house there will be five divided, three against two and two against three' (Luke 12. 51f.). Nor does Jesus come to execution, after tenaciously defending his or anyone else's right to silence. Lastly, Gethsemane shows him lapsing into terrified panic rather than thanking his Father for the honour of being martyred to save the world.

Once we have discarded comparisons taken from other martyrdoms, can we pin down a little Jesus' state of mind on the eve of execution? Three words gather up much of what can be said: failure, victimhood and obedience. He has worked and preached energetically and free from selfish and self-regarding motives. So far from renewing Israel's spiritual life, however, he emerges a failure. Almost everyone stands against him. Does he try desperately to see where he went wrong? How could he have made things go otherwise? Unlike Luke (19. 41), Mark's story does not show Jesus weeping over Jerusalem, the holy city he wished to convert. But all the same the jagged edges of pain show through. At the Last Supper he breaks the sinister news to his core group of followers that one of them has turned informer. The others will flee in panic and Peter will repeatedly disown him (14. 18–21, 27–31). These are the bald, comfortless predictions he blurts out.

Very little offsets the bleak sense of tragedy. In Mark's story Jesus only rarely expresses hope that the disciples will remember this message and continue his preaching (13. 10). The most striking reference he makes to the future of his gospel – poignantly – concerns the anonymous woman who has just anointed his body 'beforehand for burying'; 'Truly, I say to you, wherever the gospel is preached in the whole world, what she has done will be told in memory of her' (14. 8f.). Jesus dies young and all the promise of the unique preacher his disciples know threatens to come to nothing. So far from fulfilling any programme, he has not yet got anything really started. It seems that nothing will be salvaged from the ministry. The passion predictions have, of course, included the announcement that he will rise after three days. But he does not show *how* resurrection will reverse his tragic failure, and put right the mistaken refusal of his audience to follow his call for renewal. He states the fact of resurrection without unpacking its significance. Nor does Jesus ever admit that the prospect of rising from the dead somehow makes it all easier. Hebrews lets it sound almost cheerful by speaking of

Jesus, 'who for the joy that was set before him endured the cross, despising the shame' (12. 2). Robert Herrick expresses similar sentiments:

> In the hope of ease to come,
> Let's endure one Martyrdome.[12]

But Mark never shows us Jesus shrugging off the agony by some remark about 'the cross and then the crown'. (In fairness to the author of Hebrews it should be added that he also echoes the pain of Gethsemane: 'In the days of his flesh, Jesus offered up prayers and supplications, with loud cries and tears, to him who was able to save him from death' (5. 7).)

With a sparing austerity Jesus points to the value of his impending death, talking of the blood 'poured out for many' and the life given 'as a ransom for many'. In the hands of some commentators whole theologies of the redemption spring fully armed from these brief texts. Works of systematic and spiritual theology – not to mention innumerable Christian sermons – attribute to Jesus an elaborated awareness of the saving significance of his crucifixion. We can parody George Tyrrell's comment on Liberal Protestantism. The mind such writers see in Gethsemane, looking back through centuries of Christian life and worship, is only the reflection of their own thoughts on redemption, seen at the bottom of a deep well. A popular nineteenth-century author, Peter Gallwey, may serve as a scape-goat for countless others. In his meditations on the agony in the garden he writes:

> In the Soul of Jesus, there is ample space for all the different shapes of anguish. They are all within, and one does not impede another. But among them all, immeasurably more oppressive than the rest, is sin – the consciousness that He is for the present lying there, under the eyes of His Eternal Father as the Sinner, the representative of the sinful family . . . The guilt alone excepted, everything that belongs to sin, and is connected with sin, is heaped on Him. The shame, the confusion, the fear, the anguish, the intense desolation, the unbearable weight of His Father's displeasure, all this is upon Him . . . Throughout His Passion He is always, guilt excepted, the sinner's other self. He is personating sin and the sinner . . . He is crushed down to the ground by the intolerable sense of the hatred His Eternal Father bears to sin, to the sins of that guilty race to which He belongs, and which He has undertaken to represent . . . The Lord Jesus . . . lies here, identified with the sinner. For He has Himself, knowingly and deliberately, in the very strictest sense, undertaken to be his proxy.[13]

We could hardly imagine stronger claims than that! 'In the very strictest sense' Jesus *consciously* becomes victim to expiate the *entire* guilt of the *whole* human race.

One motive that often lurks behind such maximal positions is the fear that, unless Jesus himself attributed such and such an interpretation to his death, we may not be entitled to hold it for ourselves. Hence the pressure arises to allege that the doomed Jesus fully intends to put into effect redemptive schemes dreamed up by later theologians. These schemes may, of course, contain sick and distasteful elements. We can return to that in a later chapter. Here let us simply observe one point. There could be much more meaning in Jesus' death than he fully and clearly realizes when he accepts that death. Likewise there may be more meaning in a poem than the poet ever meant by it. Mark's story requires here only a simple comment. In some sense – perhaps a highly obscure sense – Jesus believes that the Father calls him to accept death for the sake of sinful men and women. Jesus says yes to that vocation of victimhood.

Then in his last hours before arrest Jesus loses his nerve, and looks for an escape route. It is not 'the dread of something after death' but the dread of death itself which wrenches him apart. He cannot join St Francis in welcoming 'sister death'. Yet he ends his terrified prayer by reaffirming his obedience. He can only push on, believing that his Father wishes him to do so. Dag Hammarskjöld's words catch the Gethsemane experience: 'Only one feat is possible – not to have run away.'[14] In the next chapter we must face what it was Jesus did not run away from.

III

CRUCIFIED

In truth, there was only *one* Christian, and he died on the cross.
                                                    Nietzsche, *Antichrist*

The painful torture wood, the most disgusting thing under the sun,
no reasonable human being should strive to exhume.
                                                    Goethe, letter to Zelter

We may wish to disregard Goethe and carefully reconstruct in
our minds the whole passion story. Any good librarian can trun-
dle forward for us a clutch of useful commentaries on the gospel
narratives, as well as painstaking books on the trial of Jesus and
endless articles on particular items – peripheral and otherwise.
We can study the accounts which acclaimed or at least accredited
scholars have put together. Yet this approach entails its own
special risk. We may end up measuring a mass of details, but
floundering over the significance of it all and even blanking out
the really unpleasant nature of Jesus' sufferings.

Ulrich Simon rightly complains that so-called critical scholarship has often rendered 'almost unreadable' many discussions of
the trial and passion of Jesus.[1] Despite the traditional language
they used and the now outmoded exegesis on which they relied,
classical works of piety often did better. They communicated an
inner picture of the passion which movingly surpassed much
later writing. We can only cry out against some latterday scholarship which – often against its best intentions – lapses into trivializ-
ing the whole story. Let us try to fend off this tendency, as we
reflect in turn on Jesus' arrest, trial and crucifixion. Historical

questions may play a subordinate role. But primarily we will read Mark's story in its own terms.

The Arrest

The passion of Jesus begins when Judas leads a party of temple police to make the arrest. Mark's narrative fails to explain the muddled and messy story of Judas' decision to turn informer. He has approached the chief priest to negotiate the terms on which he will betray his master (14. 10f.). He arranges a stealthy plot but not a stealthy assassination. He does not contract to lure Jesus off alone and stab him suddenly in a back alley of Jerusalem. Neither the chief priests nor Judas plan to have their victim killed while 'resisting arrest'. They take Jesus into custody, even though some sword-play from one of his disciples offers a fine excuse to end matters then and there (14. 43ff.). The arrest is made and the informer leaves the scene.

Mark never wavers in holding 'the elders and the chief priests and the scribes' (8. 31) responsible for initiating the passion. Early in his gospel he notes how the Pharisees and Herodians conspire to kill Jesus (3. 6). But their murderous plot comes to nothing. Some of them are 'sent' (by whom?) to trap Jesus over the issue of Roman taxation (12. 13–17), but neither Pharisees nor Herodians turn up among the killers at the end. The Sadducean priests who control the temple worship and fill the chief positions in the Sanhedrin emerge as menacing opponents from the close of chapter eight. Their opposition can look plausible. Jesus not only stages a demonstration when he enters Jerusalem (11. 1ff.), but he attacks what one might call the normal 'sacristy' business in the temple (11. 15ff.). All of this threatens public order in the capital, and may disrupt working arrangements with the Roman occupying army. The fact that Caiaphas manages to retain his office right through Pilate's years in Judea (AD 26–36) testifies to the high priest's political sense.

One can press on to argue that the Sadducean priests believe their political interests to be at stake, perhaps wrongly suspect Jesus of being a Zealot guerrilla and send their own paramilitary force of temple police to take him into custody. The arrest assumes a political character. Jesus himself seems to encourage this interpretation by insisting that he is not a lawless terrorist who can be seized only by a heavily armed force (14. 48). It all falls out quite simply. The Pharisees have opposed Jesus' *religious* message, but none of them has anything to do with his arrest, trial and execution. *Some of the Sadducees* for *purely political* reasons seize him and hand him over to the Roman authorities. The villains suddenly become humanized. They mistake a turbulent preacher for a genuine terrorist, and for motives of sensible political expediency pounce on him.

The instinct to explain things in this reasonable way, however, crashes into one perennially important line of questioning. Can we ever really separate politics and religion, even though we may refuse to reduce one to the other? In any situation – let alone first-century Palestine – may we plausibly introduce a sharp contrast between one *religiously* motivated group (for instance, the exonerated Pharisees) and another group whose *purely political*, but perfectly understandable, reasons lead them to an unjustified act of violence (for instance, some Sadducees)? These questions do not aim at alleging any guilty involvement of the Pharisees, but at undermining attempts to describe the motivation of those Sadducean priests as 'purely political'. It seems impossible to imagine how anyone, especially in that kind of situation, could ever have political motives which lacked both ethical *and* religious content. Let us take a contemporary parallel – Northern Ireland after the British troops arrived in 1969. Suppose that a group of Loyalists mistook some wandering preacher to be just another IRA terrorist ready to die for the cause, sent in members of the paramilitary UDA to arrest him, and then handed him over to the occupying army. How could we really maintain that political motives alone account perfectly well for the Loyalists' action?

Once upon a time men justified the atrocities of crusades, the executions of Tyburn, the fires of Smithfield and the activities of the Inquisition by appealing to purely religious motives. But it has become unpopular to excuse violence on such a basis. Good secular purposes sound much better, even if they sometimes have a suspiciously sacred ring like 'keeping the world safe for democracy'. Nowadays we prefer to exonerate Caiaphas and his colleagues on the grounds that they acted for reasons of state alone. However, secular and religious motives regularly show themselves thoroughly intertwined.[2] If this holds true of our advanced industrial societies where the state has achieved some authentic autonomy from religious institutions, it looks utterly anachronistic to talk of purely political motivation in the first-century world. There an alliance between the temple and palace

belonged to the natural order of things. If we chide our fore-
fathers for overlooking the secular dimension of human action,
we can fail by playing down the religious dimension.

The Trial

Once arrested, Jesus is hideously over-driven towards his death.
No tyrant takes his time before killing the innocent victim. The
story rushes us along at breathless speed in a way that Mark's
episodic narrative does not demand elsewhere. He leaves us little
leisure between Gethsemane and Golgotha. He drags us from
one item to another, without allowing time for anything to sink
in. Other writers might have used the night trial scene before
Caiaphas (14. 53ff.), and the morning hearing before Pilate (15.
1ff.) to pause for deliberate stock-taking. In fact these hurried
episodes, following one after the other, leave many issues hanging in the air.

For the first and only time in Mark's story the high priest meets
Jesus. Does his face come to life when he finally sees the prisoner?
Earlier in the gospel Herod puzzles over reports of Jesus' activity,
and decides that he is John the Baptist come back to life (6. 14–16).
Are we meant to suppose that the king recoils from the thought of
seeing again this prophet, whose head was carried through the
royal dining hall? In Luke's account Herod refuses to identify
Jesus with the murdered man, and is anxious to see him (9. 7–9).
Eventually he does (23. 6ff.). What of Caiaphas? Has he been
fretting for some time to have Jesus brought before him? Mark
refuses to fill in any background, does not even give the high
priest's name, but simply drops him into the narrative for a brief
burst of questioning. He quickly reaches his key question, 'Are
you the Christ, the Son of the Blessed?' Once he hears the
affirmative answer, he turns from the prisoner to ask other members of the council: 'Why do we still need witnesses? You have
heard his blasphemy. What is your decision?' (14. 60–64). He
makes no attempt – let alone repeated attempts – to get Jesus to
disown his claim. He neither threatens torture nor warns that
harm will come to family or friends, unless Jesus backs down.
Obviously Mark does not encourage us to speculate as to what
would happen, if Jesus refused to answer the high priest's question. Matthew, of course, represents Jesus as replying not 'I am',
but – seemingly in a somewhat evasive fashion – 'You have said
so' or 'the words are yours' (26. 64).[3] But the reaction is the same:

an accusation of blasphemy, a refusal to call further witnesses for the prosecution and the sentence of death. Neither Jesus nor the high priest argues anything out in detail.

In the morning Pilate meets Jesus for some intense moments – the only time they confront one another in Mark's story. When questioned by the Roman governor, Jesus will not positively deny a kingly mission to the Jewish nation: 'Pilate asked him, "Are you the King of the Jews?" And he answered him, "You have said so" ' (15. 2). The chief priests bring many unspecified charges against Jesus. Pilate seeks to release him, but under pressure from a crowd gives way and passes the death sentence.

Mark's narrative lets loose a swarm of historical questions. Did Caiaphas and the Sanhedrin really lack legal power to pass and execute the death penalty? Did their meeting fail to meet the accepted requirements for a sitting of that council? Was there in fact any such night trial at all? Luke reports only a brief hearing in the morning, which in any case sounds more like grand jury proceedings than a formal trial (22. 66–71). How do any of the gospel writers know what Jesus or others said and did during those episodes after his arrest, when no disciples could be present? William R. Wilson in his *The Execution of Jesus*[4] and a squad of other competent modern writers coax well-argued, if frequently divergent, answers out ot the available evidence. Let us at least try to drain off some religious implications of the gospel narratives, which historical preoccupations can lead us to neglect or even evade.

First things first. Unlike John the Baptist, Jesus does not experience simply the sequence: arrest, imprisonment, execution. Some legal proceedings intervene, as will happen with Stephen (Acts 6. 8ff.). However we care to assess the relative roles of Pilate and the priests, they inject an element of deliberateness into the story by putting Jesus on trial. Both sides confront one another to challenge, reply, and offer their final words of interpretation before Jesus is taken off to Golgotha. Both sides speak freely of God, claiming, or at least implying, divine warrant for what they say and do. Heaven must decide where truth and falsity lies in these conflicting statements.

Of course, Jesus refuses to answer some testimony brought against him (Mark 14. 60f.; 15. 5; Luke 23. 9 etc.). At times he maintains a silence that we find nowhere else, except when he writes in the sand rather than answer at once those who have hustled the adulterous woman into his presence (John 8. 6).

But through the trial scenes (and at Golgotha) Jesus does *not* endure it all dumbly like the suffering servant of Isaiah: 'He was oppressed, and he was afflicted, yet he opened not his mouth; like a lamb that is led to the slaughter, and like a sheep that before its shearers is dumb, so he opened not his mouth' (53. 7). All in all, Jesus falls somewhere between totally silent martyrs and those whose trial speeches have instructed the world. He speaks more than Margaret Clitherow (who refused to plead at all), but less than Socrates and Thomas More. No gospel offers us anything precisely like Plato's *Apology* or More's defence.

Before his martyrdom, Stephen, although speaking for the first and only time, delivers a lengthy address, which is more indictment than defence. He summarizes Israelite history as a story of resistance to the Holy Spirit (Acts 7. 2–53). In describing the legal proceedings against Jesus, Luke has three chances to insert a full-scale trial speech: in the hearings before the chief priests and scribes (22. 66–71), before Pilate (23. 1–7, 13ff.), and before Herod (23. 9–11). We could imagine Jesus anticipating the biblical lesson he gives on the road to Emmaus and interpreting 'in all the scriptures the things concerning himself' (24. 27). Or else he might let his mind run back to the time when he emerged from the desert, returned to Galilee, and began teaching 'in their synagogues, being glorified by all' (4. 14f.). Stephen-like he could summarize this ministry, noting how his audiences increasingly resisted both the appeal of his words and the promptings of the Holy Spirit. Instead, the Lukan Jesus has astonishingly little to say. He refuses to speak at all before Herod, answers in a non-committal way one question from Pilate ('Are you the King of the Jews?'), and says not much more when questioned by the chief priests. Many scholars agree that Luke feels free in Acts to fashion speeches appropriate to the occasions, and attributes them to Peter, Paul, Stephen and others. But in the case of Jesus himself Luke declines such liberties and sticks closer to the (written and oral) traditions at his disposal.

John's gospel comes closest to presenting a martyr's extended defence from the dock, but not through the passion story itself. In chapters seven and eight, as well as elsewhere in the Fourth Gospel, Jesus pleads his case and defends his claim to divine Sonship – presenting a kind of *apologia pro filiatione sua*. In fact he reverses the roles, and puts his opponents on trial for lawlessness, failure to accept the truth and intended murder: 'Did not Moses give you the law? Yet none of you keeps the law. Why do you seek to kill me?' (7. 19). No one can convict him of sin, and the case turns against them: 'If I tell the truth, why do you not believe me?' (8.46). In the great trial scene which fills chapter nine and spills over into the following chapter, a 'one-time blind beggar stands before his betters, to be badgered into denying the one thing of which he is certain. But the defendant proper is Jesus Himself, judged *in absentia*.'[5] Finally Jesus returns to the court-scene, convicts and judges those who put him and the cured beggar on trial:

> 'For judgment I came into this world, that those who do not see may see, and that those who see may become blind.' Some of the Pharisees near him heard this, and they said to him, 'Are we also blind?' Jesus said to them, 'If you were blind, you would have no guilt; but now that you say, "We see", your guilt remains' (9. 39–41).

We noted earlier how the coming passion and resurrection cast their shadow over the entire Fourth Gospel. If risky, it may also be a useful generalization to say that from the outset we can also read Jesus' discourses as a series of defence speeches. From the very beginning John anticipates the trial itself along with Jesus' crucifixion and resurrection. An excellent way to test this impression would be to read Mark's gospel up to the arrest in Gethsemane, then lay it aside and take up the Fourth Gospel as if it were nothing else but an extended and reflective version of the trial. The divine prisoner in the dock defends his identity as Son of God, indicts an unbelieving world, and names the gift of the Spirit as the aftermath of his violent death.

Our second line of comment on Jesus' trial may sound trite, but – given the way much discussion has gone – it looks necessary. It is a trip towards a pedantic dead-end to list and discuss the various charges against Jesus, as if they can be *either* political (for instance, crimes against public order or attacks on the taxation system), *or* religious in character (for instance, false claims to be Messiah or offences against the Mosaic law), but no single charge can be both political and religious. Wilson, for example, sets up such an alternative from the start: 'Was he convicted of violating Jewish religious laws or Roman civil laws or both?'[6] The presupposition comes through clearly. Religion and politics remain distinct. Secular indictments will split off neatly from accusations of religious aberrations. Roman charges will be merely civil and Jewish will be religious. Wilson correctly notes that he does not stand alone in making such a sharp distinction: 'A great many scholars have called attention to the fact that the Roman trial is political, not religious, in character and that Jesus died as a political criminal.'[7] Not only today but even more in the ancient world such a division between secular politics and religious realities will not work. Given the sacral role of the emperor, Roman trials could never be 'merely political'. Civil religion remains almost as potent a force now as it was then.

In his *Antichrist* (no. 27) Nietzsche calls Jesus 'a political criminal' precisely because of his religious and theological stance. Nietzsche rightly disowns any split between religious and secular zones.

> I fail to see against what the rebellion – as whose cause Jesus has been understood or misunderstood – may have been directed, if it was not a rebellion against the Jewish church – church exactly in the same sense in which we use the word today. It was a rebellion against 'the good and the just', against 'the saints of Israel', against the hierarchy of society – *not* against its corruption, but against caste, privilege, order and formula; it was the *disbelief* in 'higher men', the *No* to all that was priest or theologian . . . This holy anarchist, who summoned the people at the bottom, the outcastes and 'sinners', the *pariahs* within Judaism, to negate the dominant order – using language, if the Gospels could be trusted, that today, too, would still lead to Siberia – was a political criminal . . . This brought him to the cross.[8]

Finally, scholars can do such things to the trial story, that any human malice slips softly out of the picture. I am *not* wanting to revive here viciously anti-semitic nonsense, which has so often disfigured Christian thinking about Jesus' trial and death. What I have in mind is the easy plausibility with which too many writers, after (correctly) holding Pilate and only a small group of priests responsible for sending Jesus to his death, rationalize it all as an unfortunate mistake. Wilson's conclusions exemplify this trend.

On the one hand, if he refuses to 'affirm definite illegalities' in Pilate's prosecution of Jesus, he admits that 'we can obviously uncover injustice'.

> A searching examination by Pilate would have revealed that Jesus was no political pretender and that the charges against him were superficial. It is impossible to believe that Pilate made a careful and compassionate investigation into the charges against Jesus. He almost certainly judged Jesus summarily after the briefest investigation.

On the other hand, Wilson presses the case in Pilate's favour.

> His pronouncement of guilt resulted from the priests' description of Jesus' actions and from the recurrent pattern of *political turmoil* within the province. In another period, Jesus' innocence of *political plotting*

might have been obvious. But in the prolonged crisis which gripped Judaea, particularly amidst *the tension* of the Passover season, it was too easy for Pilate to identify Jesus with all those others who *had plagued him by spreading rebellion* in the country. The best guess is that Jesus also strengthened the case against himself by affirming his Messianic role, which Pilate could hardly have distinguished from *political ambition*.[9]

Two things drop clean out of sight here: the Roman governor's vicious record (which Wilson has correctly noted earlier), and the fact that Pilate headed an army of occupation on behalf of a foreign power. Friends of the Roman side could speak of 'political ambition' and 'political plotting', which increased 'the tension' and 'political turmoil' and even 'spread rebellion'. But the other side could talk of 'legitimate national aspirations' and 'resistance movements', which lead 'patriots' to 'rise in revolt' in an effort to 'drive out the enemy' and 'liberate an oppressed people'.

Wilson, likewise, treats the group of priests gently. He believes 'it much more reasonable to suppose' that they did not falsely concoct accusations, but 'built their charges around things which Jesus had actually said and done'. Thus they 'supposed, because of something which Jesus had said or done, that he opposed the payment of any tribute to Rome'.[10] Maybe. But let us hear Wilson's final judgment, before raising any challenges.

> However dishonorable it appears in our eyes, the alliance of these priests with the procurator *served a useful national purpose. They helped maintain a practicable government* without which political conditions in Judaea might have been gravely worsened. It was, after all, not these Sadducees but the Zealots who led the nation to near-extinction in the war of A.D. 66–72. The priests' cooperation with the governor, and their willingness to act as his agents when necessary, *aided in preserving the relative peace of the province.*
>
> It was this role which set them in opposition to Jesus. Despite his intentions, Jesus' activity in Jerusalem had enough of the appearance of violence, and enough promise of arousing and exciting the people, that the authorities regarded him as a threat to the restless calm of the Passover season. It is easy to imagine the worst of these priests; the execution of Jesus naturally suggests the most unprincipled villainy. But it is not in the least impossible that the Jewish national officials who sought the death of Jesus did so because they actually believed, as the Gospel of John suggests, that the death of one man might *avert political disaster for the whole nation.* He who came to Jerusalem to bring the nation nearer to God evidently lost his life because of the *mistaken fear* that he might lead it instead to destruction.[11]

This amounts more or less to an expanded version of Paul Winter's view of the Sadducees' motivation:

Faced on one side by growing popular discontent and on the other side by an overwhelming foreign power, they tried to preserve what they could of the residue of Jewish self-rule. Their fears were real, and were justified. Whether their part in the arrest of Jesus was small or great, they acted from motives they considered to serve the best interests of the nation – and *the best interests*, as so often, happened to coincide with their own.[12]

What troubles me is that all this insistently recalls the arguments used by men of property and power to justify moral outrage in every age. Let me intoduce two modern examples – the first one both tendentious and not yet focused historically, and the second one widely acceptable: the situation in Northern Ireland and the Nazi occupation of Europe. Let us first test Wilson's summary by applying it both to the Ulster ascendancy and to an officer in the British army.

> The alliance of these property-owners with the British government served a useful national purpose. They helped maintain a practicable government without which political conditions in Ulster might have gravely worsened. It was, after all, not these Protestants but the IRA terrorists who led the country to near-extinction in the war of 1969–76. The Protestant ascendancy's cooperation with the British government, and its willingness to act as that government's agent when necessary, aided in preserving the relative peace of the province.

There should be no need to continue. The apologia for the Sadducean priests might need very little alteration, if we wished to apply it to the Ulster ascendancy in general, or – let us say – to the chaplains of the Orange Lodge in particular.

Could Wilson's plea for Pilate also serve – let us say – for a British officer who hastily accepts the word of a UDA informer, believes some outsider to be an IRA terrorist, instantly subjects him to 'heavy' questioning and has him imprisoned without trial? The plea might read as follows:

> The officer's order resulted from the informer's description of this outsider's actions and from the recurrent pattern of political turmoil within the province. In another period, the outsider's innocence of terrorist activity might have been obvious. But in the prolonged crisis which gripped Ulster, particularly amidst the tension of the Orangemen's marches, it was too easy for the officer to identify the outsider with all those others who had plagued him by spreading rebellion in the country. The best guess is that the outsider also strengthed the case against himself by belief in a united Ireland, which the officer could hardly have distinguished from IRA involvement.

Let me turn from this tendentious example to the story of

Czechoslovakia, France and other countries occupied by the German forces during the Second World War. 'Serving a useful national purpose', 'maintaining a practicable government', 'preserving the relative peace of the country' and 'trying to preserve the residue of national rule' – men used these reasons to justify a collaboration that entailed rounding up innocent Jews to be trucked away to extermination camps. Wilson's words could easily be pressed into service to defend members of Vichy governments and other puppet regimes.

> It is easy to imagine the worst of these men: the extermination of Jews naturally suggests the most unprincipled villainy. But it is not in the least impossible that these national officials who sought the death of the Jews did so because they actually believed that the death of this group might avert political disaster for the whole nation.

Could Winter's reflection also apply to this wartime situation? 'Whether their part in the arrest and deportation of Jews was small or great, these collaborators acted from motives they considered to serve the best interests of the nation – and *the best interests*, as so often, happened to coincide with their own.' We need not ascribe to such collaborators 'frenzied bloodthirstiness' against the Jews, nor accuse them of being 'rabidly intent' on the extermination of the Jewish population.[13] A certain moral indifference can impel men to defend their 'interests', even when it means deliberately co-operating in murder. There are few more potent motives for rationalizing atrocities than power and property.

In discussing the trial story, Wilson finds Mark's account historically incredible when it reports how members of the Sanhedrin taunted and abused Jesus. He writes: 'One must have considerable contempt for the quality of the nation's leaders in order to accept such a tradition. Their treatment of Jesus – spitting on him, striking him, yelling insults – is such as we would expect from the worst rabble of Jerusalem.'[14] One might also argue that some of the things seen in Max Ophuls' *The Sorrow and the Pity* and reported from the Stormont Parliament are such as we would expect from the worst rabble of Paris or Belfast. Of course, we should not foster 'considerable contempt for the quality' of Ulster and French leaders. But can we also err through a deep reluctance to admit real malice in such ruling classes?

Clearly we would need to touch up only slightly the plea for Pilate before applying it to some Nazi official in occupied Europe, who – let us say – receives a report against a man who did not in fact belong to the resistance, made a summary investigation, and then ordered the man to be shot at once. Partisan activity – one could argue – had thrown the country into turmoil. It was too easy to identify this prisoner with all those others who plagued the German forces by spreading guerrilla attacks. The prisoner strengthened the case against himself by affirming his belief in God's justice, which the Nazi official could not distinguish from an insult to Hitler's policies.

What I have just argued applies to vicious acts of violence committed anywhere. That includes my own country and my own church. The heart of the matter is this. I wish to part company with any versions of Jesus' trial and condemnation which parallel the arguments used by countless men of power and privilege to justify their moral outrages. Professor Wilson is not only a careful scholar – correctly citing other writers who support his case at different points – but also communicates the sense of being a deeply good person. I shrink from my remarks being taken as yet another dreary example of spiteful debates among theologians. Nevertheless, I find deeply disturbing implications in putting Jesus' condemnation finally down to the 'mistaken fear' of some temple officials and Pilate's error in a crisis. Such a view comes within hailing distance of explaining away evil violence in contemporary society and even in our own lives. The arguments Wilson and others use to exonerate Pilate and the priests need only a little touching up, if one wishes to use them in that way.

There is no need to understand Pilate and the priests as necessarily deformed persons. If we cannot get rid of them that way, we may want to ask: How could they have done it? Before the crucifixion Pilate's wife warned her husband that she had been deeply troubled in her dreams. Did Caiaphas and Pilate sleep badly afterwards? Were they haunted for years by what they had done? After all, Jesus' fate quickly drove Judas to suicide. We might ask similar questions about Henry VIII when Thomas More's severed head was stuck on London Bridge, about the English soldiers after Joan of Arc's ashes had been flung into the Seine, or about the Gestapo agents who hanged Dietrich Bonhoeffer. But most of those who kill martyrs look neither totally monstrous beforehand nor deeply haunted afterwards. From the little we see of Pilate and the priests in the gospel story – or for that matter can learn of them elsewhere – their value-systems seem coherent, intelligible and even uncomfortably like our own. They are not ridiculous people, but have plenty of successes to their credit. I suspect that Pilate, Caiaphas and Judas leave us uneasy about the possible results of our common human malice, and even terrified by the dark evil that sleeps in us all. In Mark's story Jesus looks extremely vulnerable. Pilate and the others hardly have to ignore any traditional safeguards or ordinary defences before killing him. If the normal limits came down, what would our greed allow us to do? How far would we go to maintain or acquire power, property and privilege?

The Crucifixion

With the power of the Roman Empire behind him, Pilate ordered Jesus to be crucified. Normally only rebels or runaway slaves need fear that their lives could be torn from them by this hideous combination of impalement and display. No matter what their offences, Roman citizens were rarely, if ever, crucified. When Paul left Jerusalem for the last time, he was under an armed guard (Acts 23. 23ff.), but crucifixion did not loom up ahead of him. It could be no more than the most remote of possibilities. When Jesus walked out of Jerusalem for the last time, the Roman soldiers formed an execution squad – not a friendly and heavily armed guard hurrying him away from a dangerous situation.

At Golgotha Jesus experienced an obscenely painful and ugly death. By the normal standards of crucifixion, he died rather quickly and not after an agony drawn-out interminably (Mark 15. 43–45). Even so, this torture killing was horrifyingly different from the quick hanging by which Bonhoeffer died or the dulling hemlock which carried Socrates away. Not everyone cares to think of the ancient Romans as sadists who liked to inflict frightful cruelties with sheer delight. Nevertheless, crucifixion happened frequently within the normal framework of their society. If we refuse to call this method of execution unbearable and unspeakable in our horror, it gets very close to that. Like so many others Jesus was pinned up to writhe for hours in extreme pain. We must never lose sight of the leisurely cruelty of his execution.

Mark (followed by Matthew), Luke and John offer us three versions of the crucifixion – like the same tragic plot told repeatedly by different people. It is not a case of their realizing that, since Calvary lacks mass appeal, they must somehow fashion an appealing hero out of the crucified Jesus. They simply try to cope with the shame and horror of it all.

In Luke weeping women see Jesus pass like a noble martyr to his death. Despite the pain his thoughts go out to others: these women, those who crucify him and a criminal crucified alongside him. He warns the women, 'Daughters of Jerusalem, do not weep for me, but weep for yourselves and for your children' (23. 28). When fastened to the cross, his first prayer is: 'Father, forgive them; for they know not what they do' (23. 34). He comforts the good thief with the promise, 'Truly, I say to you, today you will be with me in Paradise' (23. 43). With a last prayer he is gone: 'Father, into thy hands I commend my spirit' (23. 46).

John ignores the mocking by some bystanders at the crucifixion, and like Luke does not include the cry of dereliction. He wishes us to know that Jesus looks back and thinks at the end, 'I've completed my mission' (19. 30). With Luke, John pictures the dying Jesus as also looking forward in concern for others. He commits his widowed mother to the care of the beloved disciple (19. 26f.).

In Mark's account, however, Jesus neither glances back to what he has achieved in his ministry, nor looks forward with some cry of hope, 'Father, I'm coming home'. The appalling present situation blots out everything else: 'My God, my God, why hast thou forsaken me?' (15. 34). Many exegetes and theologians offer explanations which do their best to mitigate the chilling loneliness of that cry. It is the only time in Mark's gospel that Jesus uses words of scripture to address his Father in prayer. It is the only question Jesus asks after his arrest. Caiaphas and Pilate interrogate him. But he questions no one before this one and only word from the cross. His question suggests a complete isolation. His family, his village, the people of Galilee, its ruler, the Pharisees, the Sadducees, the people of Jerusalem, the core group of disciples whom he hand-picked – everyone has left him to suffer a slow and obscene death at the hands of the occupying army. And now he shrieks out that God too has left him. Before Jesus reaches the moment of death, Luke and John assure us that some women and even one or two men attend to mourn the crucifixion. But Mark, as it were, lets Jesus die utterly alone. It is only then that he mentions Mary Magdalene and other friendly bystanders (15. 40f.), as well as the conversion of the man who led the execution squad. We might think of asking: How could you take part in a thing like that without feeling very badly about it afterwards? Mark bypasses any post-crucifixion remorse, and makes the Roman centurion the first person on earth to penetrate the divine incognito of Jesus: 'Truly this man was the Son of God'(15. 39). Once Jesus dies, Mark elevates our painful emotions, and in so doing calms them. But not before.

It is often said that death puts a stamp on life. We may measure a man's life by his death. But it is also true that we must measure our lives against another death, a crucifixion at 'the place of a skull'. What can put a stamp on our lives is our willingness to look steadily at the man who screamed out his prayer in the moment of death, *'Eloi, Eloi, lama sabachthani?'*

IV

AGENTS OF THE CRUCIFIXION

The cross of Christ has cast its shadow over all time.

Karl Rahner, *The Eternal Year*

Jesus will be in agony to the end of the world. We must not sleep during that time.

Pascal, *Pensées*

The life of Jesus ended in a shocking and shameful way. Is it possible to get behind this death to explain it, or at least to cope with its vicious meaninglessness? Any response will have to be deeply shaped by our main source, the New Testament. Can we align ourselves with some important ways in which the imagination of the first Christians worked on the event of the crucifixion? Three texts from St Paul, the earliest New Testament writer, suggest a theme around which to begin organizing our reflections – namely, the agents involved in producing Calvary.

In Galatians the apostle speaks of 'the Son of God, who loved me and gave himself for me' (2. 20). Earlier he attributes the crucifixion to 'the Jews, who killed both the Lord Jesus and the prophets' (I Thess. 2. 15). In his masterpiece Paul acknowledges that God the Father 'did not spare his own Son but gave him up for us all' (Rom. 8. 32). Thus he points towards (1) Jesus himself, (2) a group of human beings, and (3) God the Father when the question arises: Who intended that the crucifixion should take place? In parenthesis we can note how Mark, the first evangelist, also produces three such answers. (1) Jesus died freely: 'The Son

of man came . . . to give his life' (10. 45). (2) The passion story
obviously indicates how a number of men joined forces to execute
Jesus. (3) The first passion prediction has a predetermined ring
about it, implying that God (the Father) took the initiative in
arranging for the death on Calvary: 'The Son of man *must* suffer
many things . . . and be killed' (8. 31).

It may look impossible to harmonize into any coherence these
various agents whom Paul (and Mark) hold responsible for the
death on Calvary. Let us try to make some sense out of these
diverging texts. If we wish to examine what happened *through*
Jesus, we need first to ask what happened *to* Jesus. The previous
chapters have, of course, approached that question from various
angles. But now we should steadily face the issue: Who intended
it all, why do these intentions matter and how can we relate the
different agents involved?

Jesus' Intentions

Theoretically two extremes are possible when we examine the
role of Jesus. On the one hand, we could argue that there is no
connection at all between what Jesus intended to do and what
actually overtook him. Such a thesis could go as far as to assert
that Jesus positively tried to escape death and had to be dragged
screaming to the cross. On the other hand, we might maintain
that his intent coincided exactly with what happened to him and
through him. Could the catastrophe of the crucifixion have been
(A) *either* totally unexpected, unintended and even unwanted, *or*
(B) totally foreseen and premeditated?

(A)   We might try to make peace with the first possibility by
alleging that, through some mysterious arrangement of divine
providence, a man could in fact have saved the human race
without actually expecting, intending, or even wanting to do so.
That would sound like a principle shaped by *The Imitation of
Christ*: 'It is better to bring about the world's redemption than
know how to define it.' But, as we have seen, the gospels shut out
any chance of taking the crucifixion as an utterly unexpected and
unintended disaster, which swept Jesus away like a bolt from the
Judean blue. His conflicts with menacing opponents, his reflections on the fate of prophets, the passion predictions, the Last
Supper and the agony in the garden prevent us from holding the
passion to be merely something which *happened to* Jesus. We
would have to argue that none of this material had any basis in

Jesus' life. Besides, a completely unexpected and unwanted death would make Calvary look like a meaningless catastrophe turned to his own purposes by an outsider God. It is not that we need to assert that the value of the crucifixion resided wholly – or even principally – in the conscious intentions behind what Jesus did and suffered. Nevertheless, if we strike out any deliberate purpose on his part, we make him into a totally passive or even unwilling victim, whose murder God picked in an arbitrary fashion to serve for the redemption of mankind. Such a thesis maintains an extreme separation between (1) the order of being and (2) the order of knowledge. On the level of what is and what is done, Jesus' death brought salvation to the world. Yet he neither knew nor intended anything of this in advance! Even St Paul, although he usually bypasses any discussion of what goes through the mind of Jesus before the crucifixion, cannot confine simply to the order of being and cries out: 'He loved me and gave himself for me.' It seems both historically correct and theologically sound to acknowledge that Jesus went willingly and to some extent 'knowingly' to his death.

(B) In chapter II we raised in a preliminary way the question which could lead us to the other extreme: How far did Jesus intend the crucifixion? A totally premeditated death could, of course, go to the point of being suicide. Did Jesus then save the world through a self-inflicted death? Here we should resolutely refuse to accept the easy explanation that in his divine identity Jesus had absolute rights over life and death – his own case included. Such an explanation does not shrink from admitting that we are redeemed by the incarnate Word resolving on his own death and then taking his own life. To put matters bluntly, this comes to redemption by the suicide of God.

The gospel story itself forces us to pull back from accepting such a thesis. Jesus neither passed sentence on himself nor carried out his own execution. Socrates swallowed the poison after being convicted by his fellow-Athenians. French officers could shoot themselves when condemned to death by court martial. But Jesus neither nailed himself to the cross, nor asked any earthly or heavenly being to do this for him. Angels ministered to him in the wilderness (Mark 1. 13), an 'angel from heaven' appeared to strengthen him in Gethsemane (Luke 22. 43), and he insisted that his Father could send him 'more than twelve legions of angels' if he needed such reinforcements (Matt. 26. 53). But the evangelists do not picture Jesus asking for any angelic executioner to ensure that the crucifixion takes place. No such destroying angel came to strike down the first-born son of Mary.

The letter to the Hebrews develops, of course, the theme of Jesus as both high priest *and victim*. Once for all and one for all, this priest made a sacrifice for sins by offering himself (9. 14, 26; 10. 12 etc.). Drawing on the ritual practised in the Jerusalem temple, the letter pictures Jesus entering 'into the Holy Place, taking not the blood of goats and calves but his own blood' (9. 12). But the writer soon assures his readers that he speaks – not literally of some ceremony carried out in an earthly sanctuary – but figuratively of an invisible entry into heaven itself (9. 24). Others butchered Jesus on Calvary. He did not strictly victimize himself by shedding his own blood. When the author of Hebrews refers to the crucifixion, he warns that lapsing from Christian faith amounts to joining those men who put Jesus to death: 'If they commit apostasy', 'they crucify the Son of God on their own account' (6. 6). Jesus offered himself, but that does not mean that he crucified himself. In Arthur Miller's *Death of a Salesman* Willy Loman passes from selling things to selling himself. After failing his family for years, he arranges for his own death, so that they can live from the insurance. Jesus did not pass from selling his message to selling himself for the sake of others. Someone else sold him. He was not his own victim in that sense. Nor did he seize a sword in Gethsemane, fall on it, and surrender his life in sacrifice to the Father – thus snatching from those who thought they had cornered him the chance of killing him for themselves.

If we back away from interpreting the crucifixion as suicide, how far did Jesus' self-involvement with his own death go? A phrase suggested to me by John Cowburn – 'willing by acceptance' – offers the right middle-ground between the two extremes we have been considering.[1] Jesus willed his violent death by accepting it. He did not positively seek death, but submitted when death found him out. In short, Calvary amounted to self-surrender without self-destruction.

Broadly speaking, what one 'wills by acceptance' may fall into either of two classes: (1) the things which one has in no sense caused, and (2) those things which one has in some way provoked. Being born with a deformity, growing up with a Galilean accent, having *this* couple for one's parents, and living at *this* point in world history – such factors form the typical 'given' of a human existence which the individual must learn to concur with, even though it is all simply thrust upon him. Yet there may be other things one does not want to happen but which arise as a result of one's freely chosen course of action. A prophet's message can evoke a clamour of hatred which eventually leads to his murder. He does not intend that his audience react in this fashion, but out of obedience to his vocation he continues to preach, and then has to accept the violent death he has in some sense brought about. He found it necessary to act and refused to give way, even though his action set him on a deadly collision course. An heroic prophet can thus become the tragic victim of a killing at which in a way he has himself connived. The crucifixion falls into this second class of events willed by acceptance. At least indirectly Jesus brought about the deadly situation by continuing his ministry, confronting his critics and going to Jerusalem.

Here we need to part company with the milder version Aquinas offers (in the third part of his *Summa*) to explain how Jesus caused his death indirectly. He did so by not preventing it, even though he could have prevented it. St Thomas suggests the analogy of someone who looks up, sees the rain coming into his room, but fails to get up and close the window (qu. 47, a. 1). However, this explanation falls short of the gospel story. Far from simply deciding *not to prevent* his opponents from killing him, Jesus *provoked* their hostility. His ministry and message (admittedly, to his dismay) *caused* the hostility to rain down on him. It would have stopped, if he had shifted and backed off from his mission.

Jesus was not only the victim but also the architect of his own fate. His 'willing by acceptance' amounted to bringing it all down on himself. This raises the question: Did Jesus *sin* by provoking the power, fear and greed of others to the point that they killed him? Few writers follow Nietzsche by answering that question in the affirmative.[2] Some, however, get close to suggesting that a 'fatal flaw' – perhaps a defect in tactics – put Jesus on the cross. He failed to make things perfectly clear, allowed men in power to misinterpret his intentions, and thus bore some responsibility for their action in killing him. By pinning an error of judgment on Jesus, such an approach makes him somewhat to blame, and represents the human agents of his crucifixion as themselves victims of a regrettable but understandable mistake. In this view Jesus may have been the ultimately good man, but he did not suffer the utterly unmerited misfortune. This view refuses to admit simply that it was Jesus' virtue and not his fault that brought worldly disaster on him.

Will such a sub-Nietzschean explanation work? It means alter-
ing John's text to read, 'Which of you convicts me of error?' (8.
46), then finding some error and answering the question in the
affirmative. Jesus should not have engaged in such a provocative
style of ministry before a public so accustomed to – and even so
prone to – savage violence. He demanded too much, did not
observe the rule 'live and let live', and failed to show himself
normal, well balanced and inoffensive. How could he have failed
to realize that no authorities could run a temple, if wandering
preachers were going to burst in and make prophetic protests
against 'sacristy' business? He should have explained carefully to
Pilate that his preaching of God's kingdom did not really threaten
to trigger off a burst of guerrilla attacks. We could take each of
these and other alleged errors, and use what evidence we have to
argue matters out in detail. Yet rather than adopt such a
piecemeal approach, it may be more useful to point out where the
real trouble lies. We face *a fatally flawed world*. Jesus reached out
and tested society. He was not moderate and accommodating.
He called on men and women caught in false and compromising
situations to break free and serve God in honest obedience. But
his society turned on him to find him guilty of the ultimate and
unforgivable crime of being himself. Every society can show itself
as sick as his by destroying surpassing individuals at the height of
their powers. It makes such individuals suffer both for what they
are and for what they try to do. One who goes hunting for
some fatal flaw in Jesus is, in fact, making excuses for our world.
We all live in a fatally flawed society, and it will always be like
that.

If we agree to describe Jesus as 'willing' his violent death by
accepting that fate when thrust upon him, what did he intend to
achieve through dying? What did he expect from the crucifixion?
Of course, the value of Calvary may go beyond the values he
consciously died for. The actual results may far outstrip what he
intended to do. Here, as elsewhere, we cannot turn the historical
Jesus and his intentions into the *sole* criterion for interpreting the
crucifixion or anything else. The risen Christ himself, enlighten-
ment by the Holy Spirit and their own reflections guided the early
Christians in discovering fresh meaning in the brutalizing and
agonizing death outside Jerusalem. Neverthelesss, we dare not
treat Jesus' pilgrimage to the crucifixion as a mere prolegomena,
a piece of human history that lacks interest for us. Once we
acknowledge the voluntary quality of his death as significant, we

must press on to ask: What did he expect to achieve through martyrdom.

Apropos of T. S. Eliot's *Murder in the Cathedral*, Raymond Williams remarks that 'the centre of the play is the consciousness of the martyr'.[3] One *might* risk applying this description to the Fourth Gospel. Yet John offers such a special mixture of reminiscence and theological reflection, that the historical Jesus appears fused almost inextricably with the dramatic and divine Christ – the object of the evangelist's faith. Efforts to push beyond the consciousness of the Johannine Christ to the earthly original remain tentative in the extreme. In the case of the synoptic gospels no one can allege that their centre is the consciousness of the martyr. In trying to use them to recapture what Jesus intended to happen through his violent death, we are largely pulling at broken strings. Mark 10. 45 suggests an identification with a suffering servant atoning for man's sins: 'The Son of man also came not to be served but to serve, and to give his life as a ransom for many.' But do these words in fact come from the historical Jesus himself? The Last Supper narrative interprets Calvary as mediating a new covenant: 'This is my blood of the covenant, which is poured out for many' (Mark 14. 24). But how far has the liturgy of the post-Easter church shaped this text? In Jerusalem Jesus provoked dangerous opposition by driving out of the temple precincts vendors and money-changers – associates, if not in fact relatives of the priests who ran the temple. The whole incident may have looked like a minor disturbance of the peace, perhaps 'little more than a brawl in an Eastern bazaar'.[4] All the same, the event belongs to the history of the earthly Jesus. What did he intend, however, by this prophetic action? Was it meant to signify the end of the old order and the beginning of a new order to be initiated definitively through his death? Our difficulty then is this. Where the *words* clearly interpret the crucifixion (Mark 10. 45; 14. 24), we may seriously doubt whether they derive from Jesus himself. Where we can be confident that some *action* took place (the cleansing of the temple), we cannot pin down exactly what Jesus might have intended to imply about his destiny through engaging in this action.

The evidence plainly teases and troubles us. Nevertheless, we need not despair of probing the historical Jesus' intentions and proceed to renounce even what was briefly argued in chapter II. A couple of expressions gather up much of what can be said: (1) obedience towards the Father, and (2) a resolution to liberate and reconcile sinful men and women. The Gethsemane story shows Jesus overcoming a crisis of obedience, an obedience which in any case was called into question when he freely went up to Jerusalem. He was neither threateningly summoned to appear in Jerusalem, nor tricked into going there. Two motives pressed him to make that last journey: (a) the general duty acknowledged by other pious Jews to celebrate the Passover in Jerusalem, and (b) his particular vocation to continue bearing prophetic witness to God's coming rule. The situation could only have looked threatening. Conscious obedience was in play. For all their differences, Paul, John and the author of Hebrews show themselves at one with the synoptic gospels in highlighting obedience when they treat the crucifixion. The resolution to be absolutely obedient to his vocation cost Jesus his life. Previously his obedience expressed itself through activity, but in the passion the initiative passed out of his hands. His obedience then took the form of accepting the victim-role thrust upon him.

During the ministry Jesus gave himself with prodigal energy to the tasks of *reconciling* and *liberating* sinful men and women. When he spoke of being among them 'as one who serves' (Luke 22. 27), his role went beyond that of the best and most bountiful humanitarian. A willingness to lose his life (Mark 8. 35) and act as the servant of all (Mark 9. 35) drove him to associate with prostitutes, taxation agents and other marginal groups. They placed little value on themselves and were considered unclean by respectable society (Mark 2. 15–17). Jesus played the role of divine physician by expressing forgiveness and love towards these 'sick' people. Even supposing that he never outraged 'the righteous' by literally pronouncing *words* of absolution (Mark 2. 5–7), through his *action* of eating and drinking with outcasts he brought them pardon. By admitting into his company at table the people who were obviously and openly guilty, he received them into God's company. Those meals enacted prophetically the eschatological banquet, at which the community of the saved will include such sinners. Jesus liberated them from the status of religious pariahs, reconciled them with God and brought them into a new community. He knew we need a great deal of convincing that our happiness is not based on, nor conditioned by, our innocence. God offers his intimate friendship to the apparently irredeemable.

It would be strange to think that the approach of the passion abruptly corroded and destroyed Jesus' desire to continue liberating and reconciling sinners. Is it too much to suppose that, as the chance to play this role actively slipped away from him, he interpreted his destiny through a current Jewish idea: the just man who represents others and expiates their sins through his death?[5] He who had shown himself the servant of all accepted the vocation to become the suffering servant for all. The idea was in the air: his contemporaries recognized that through martyrdom a just person could die 'for many'. During his ministry Jesus spent himself on the work of reconciling and liberating sinners. It would seem almost unaccountably odd that the vicarious value of his impending death never occurred to him. *Once he came to expect a violent death*, how could he have failed to be concerned with its atoning power.

The ideas I have been feeling after could easily be perverted into attributing to Jesus a full-blown soteriology. We should rather think of an *implicit soteriology*, and allow for an advance to the explicit theologies of salvation found in Paul, Hebrews, John and later writers. Nowadays many scholars point to the implicit christology, which can be traced in the ministry of Jesus and which helped to give rise to the explicit christology of the early Christians.His preaching implied, for instance, a unique claim to authority. At times he called the Mosaic law into question, put himself above that law and spoke in God's place. Deciding for or against Jesus became tantamount to deciding for or against the divine rule. He maintained flatly that men's attitude towards him would determine their fate before God: 'Every one who acknowledges me before men, the Son of man also will acknowledge before the angels of God; but he who denies me before men will be denied before the angels of God' (Luke 12. 8f.). The high christology of the post-Easter church had its roots in what the earthly Jesus implied about himself. An understanding of his saving work unfolded in a similar way. The largely implicit soteriology attributed to Jesus in the synoptic gospels grew into an explicit soteriology. He who had never called himself by that name came to be worshipped as the 'Saviour', who 'gave himself for us to redeem us from all iniquity' (Titus 3. 13f.). In the next chapters we will examine some key themes in this developed soteriology.

The Human Agents

If Jesus 'willed by acceptance' his violent death, what of those who actively took his life from him? Many sermons, hymns and prayers describe Pilate, Caiaphas and Judas as mankind's representatives. A Roman governor, a Jewish priest and a follower of Jesus stood in for us and did the deed. The Good Friday liturgy addresses its reproaches to contemporary congregations, evokes their common experience of guilt, and associates them with the historical persons who two thousand years ago literally put Jesus to death. We share the responsibility with our representatives from the first century! The liturgy presents the crucifixion as a public enactment of destruction, which involves all social groups and every individual.

Nevertheless, does it make sense to allege some collective guilt, and maintain that *we all* somehow had a hand in the crucifixion? The New Testament never asserts that all men and women should be considered the agents of Jesus' execution. This death has implications and value for the whole of mankind. But no New Testament writer scans the limits of the known world to maintain that all those people – from the Scots to the Indians and from the Germans to the Africans – bore responsibility for Calvary. Luke reports that at Pentecost the 'devout men' gathered in Jerusalem 'from every nation under heaven' included 'Parthians and Medes and Elamites and residents of Mesopotamia, Judea and Cappadocia, Pontus and Asia, Phrygia and Pamphylia, Egypt and the parts of Libya belonging to Cyrene, and visitors from Rome, both Jews and proselytes, Cretans and Arabians' (Acts 2. 5–11). When Peter stands up to explain how a group of Galileans could suddenly break into a range of foreign languages, he goes on to tax his audience with responsibility for the death on Calvary: 'Jesus. . . you crucified and killed by the hands of lawless men' (v. 23). But he makes his charge against the 'men of Israel' (v. 22) or 'all the house of Israel' (v. 36) – *not* against 'all who dwell in Jerusalem', the visitors who had come from 'far off' (vv. 14, 39). Peter expects that his whole audience needs to repent and seek forgiveness for their sins (v. 38). But neither he nor anyone else in the New Testament rushes to blame the Parthians, Medes, Cretans and other known contemporaries in that first-century world for having been somehow present in Jerusalem to put Jesus on the cross. Still less does the New Testament attribute such responsibility to either past or future generations of men and women, to those already dead or those not yet born.

For his part, Paul betrays remarkably little interest in naming *any* human agents for the crucifixion. Apart from mentioning briefly 'the Jews' (I Thess. 2. 15), and 'the rulers of this age' (I Cor.

2. 8), he never cites the Sadducean priests, Judas, Pilate or any other participants in the passion story. Paul's 'rulers of this age' seem not to be human authorities but wicked spirits who hold the world in slavery. He insistently reminds his converts, 'Christ was crucified for you'. But he never tells them, 'You put him there'. If Paul adopts traditional terminology to declare that Christ died 'for us', he understands that this death took place 'for our benefit' but not 'at our hands'. Paul blasts away at the sins of those early Christians, pressing a wide range of sacred and profane arguments into service. At one point Paul laments that the moral standards of the Corinthian community have fallen below those of ordinary pagans (I Cor. 5. 2f.). At another point he denounces fornication as unworthy of those who have received the Holy Spirit (I Cor. 6. 19). But he nowhere adopts a line of motivation found in Hebrews (6. 6): 'Your sins mean siding with Pilate and Caiaphas. Your sins nail Christ to the cross.' Paul tenaciously argues for the disturbing conclusion: 'All have sinned' (Rom. 3. 23). Here and elsewhere he maintains universal sinfulness, but he never alleges universal responsibility for the crucifixion. God has taken the initiative in reconciling to himself a hostile and sinful mankind: 'While we were enemies we were reconciled to God by the death of his Son' (Rom. 5. 10). But Paul does not attribute that death to the hostility of those who had rejected God's friendship. The text from Romans fails to read: 'Although we were the enemies who had caused the death of his Son, we were reconciled to God by that same death.'

Nevertheless, the disturbing reproaches of the Good Friday liturgy rightly imply that we are all spiritually inter-connected with Pilate, Caiaphas and Judas. Those men played out a psychodrama, in which we can recognize our archetypal sins of greed, pride and self-concern. We have no inbuilt guarantee that we could not be as ruthless, treacherous and brutal. Given their chance, even our laziness and cowardice could produce as much evil as the greedy force and cunning of others. After quoting W. H. Auden's line from *Spain* ('The conscious acceptance of guilt in the necessary murder'), Raymond Williams suggests: 'It is interesting to imagine the line rewritten as "the conscious acceptance of guilt in the necessary killing" and then ask how many people, in reality, dissent from this. Most people I know, and most humane liberals I have heard of, accept killing in this sense again and again.'[6] Is there after all not such a wide gap between any of us and the historical agents of the crucifixion? Common sense may tug at our elbow and tell us that it is absurd to apply Williams's comment to Calvary. Who would accept the crucifixion as 'the necessary killing' and consciously accept responsibility for it? Of course, each of us has no conscience to examine but his own. But do I recognize in myself degrading flaws that – given the necessary circumstances – could even make me join forces with those who directly killed Jesus?

If 'conscious acceptance of *guilt*' seems too strong, must we at least speak of the 'conscious acceptance of *shame*'? The brother of a murderer might properly deny any guilty share in the evil deed. But he would be less than human not to feel shame at what his brother has done. We stand in solidarity with Caiaphas, Pilate and Judas. We can do no less than acknowledge the shameful truth and admit to ourselves, 'These are my brothers'.

Nevertheless, accepting collective shame but denying the collective guilt and protesting one's own innocence will not do. We share in the irrational evil of those who killed Jesus. If the *good effects* of Calvary spread to all generations, the *moral malice* that struck Jesus down wears a common face. In his death Jesus acts for the good of all mankind. The human agents also act larger than life. Their Roman or Jewish identities are no more than a thin veil through which man's mysterious passion for evil is plainly visible. They represent us *in* our moral indifference, as much as Jesus represents us *for* our ultimate good. We share in the *Sin* of Pilate, Caiaphas and Judas, even though it may flare up into a variety of personal *sins*. Only one Roman soldier drives a spear into Jesus' corpse, but the words John quotes from Zechariah aim at everyone: 'They shall look on him whom they have pierced' (19. 37). Only those Romans and Jews directly involved bear the guilt for the crucifixion. Yet universal solidarity in the radical disorder of sin allows us to speak of a collective guilt shared by all. The crucifixion has all the appearance of an event for which particular men took responsibility, but which at the same time was outside their control. It was under the control of that primal lust for evil which lays its hand on everyone.

God the Father

All in all, we might hope to cope with the crucifixion, if we had to deal only with the human agents who brought it about – on the one hand, the rulers of this world who take direct responsibility for the killing and, on the other hand, Jesus himself who obediently accepts his savage victimization. But, as we saw at the beginning of this chapter, Paul and Mark announce that God the Father took the initiative in sending his Son to death. Other New Testament authors agree (John 3. 16; Luke 24. 26). But what kind of a God is this who sets his slaughtered Son at the heart of the universe? In recent years one popular poster has reminded us that 'the glory of God is man fully alive'. But it seems that at least once the glory of God was a uniquely great man fully dead. Another contemporary poster proclaims: 'To believe in God is to know that all the rules will be fair and that there will be wonderful surprises.' Jesus believed in God – to put it mildly. Yet if his death took place by 'the definite plan and foreknowledge of God' (Acts 2. 23; cf. 3. 18), we appear to be dealing with a God intent on killing his incarnate Son – not on keeping fair rules or providing wonderful surprises. The more the New Testament writers speak of a divine initiative in the crucifixion, the less easy it becomes to pull back from picturing God as mercilessly planning for his Son's death by torture killing. Paul edges us towards thinking of such divine treachery by his choice of verb: God 'gave his Son up' (Rom. 8. 32), just as the arch-betrayer, Judas, 'gave his master up'.[7] The divine Traitor was the invisible counterpart to the human traitor.

In tackling this difficulty, Thomas Aquinas correctly admits that handing an innocent man over to such a death could only be wickedly cruel – if this happened *against his will*. However, so far from having the victim dragged screaming to the cross, God the Father both inspired Jesus with courage and love and waited on his free decision to suffer for mankind.[8]

Furthermore, we can help ourselves here with the notion of an 'act of God'. The New Testament authors inherited from the Jewish religion the conviction that certain events in Israel's total history should be attributed to special divine intervention. They added to this list the whole history of Jesus, his crucifixion included. By naming the execution on Calvary an 'act of God', no one intends to deny that it is also an 'act of man' – an act in which both Jesus himself and other men took part. A finely meshed array of human causality was obviously at work in bringing the crucifixion about, just as in the sixth century BC thousands of human agents produced the Babylonian captivity. Such 'acts of God' presuppose, rather than exclude, human activity. This human activity may be virtuous and heroic to a unique degree. However, besides figures like Jeremiah and Jesus, the other human agents involved may behave with savage brutality and callous unconcern. To call some event an 'act of God' is in no way to deny that thoroughly evil choices may have caused the same event, if we view it as an 'act of man'.

Nevertheless, to characterize the crucifixion or any other event as an 'act of God' is to allege a special divine presence and activity. In such events of human history God engages himself in a higher degree. At those points God reveals more of his concerns and interests than he does elsewhere. He does not always engage himself with the world and all its history in exactly the same degree. He enters into some events in ways that show his hand.

It follows that such 'acts of God' convey their special religious messages. Thus the death of Jesus requires that men and women acknowledge the divine claim being made, take certain decisions and adopt particular patterns of action. Paul goes beyond saying that God 'gave up his Son' to add that this happened 'for us all'. God was after something in allowing this brutal death to occur. He wished to wake in us some appropriate responses. He was no Judas-God, intent on playing traitor for lonely reasons of his own. The divine concern for mankind surrounds the raw statement that 'He did not spare his own Son': *'If God is for us, who is against us?* He who did not spare his own Son but gave him up *for us all, will he not also give us all things with him*?' (Rom. 8. 31f.). As an 'act of God' Calvary tolerates for Paul no other conclusion than that God is on our side.

As always, however, 'acts of God' are never unambiguously so. We may fail to see these events for what they are. No one forces us to attend and agree that *here* God has truly shown his hand. The crucifixion does not shout its message at the world. This 'act of God' leaves us free to take the risk of acknowledging that God engaged himself on our behalf on the death of Jesus.

Everyone can agree that both (1) Jesus himself and (2) some other men collided to bring about the execution on Calvary. No matter how they assign responsibility and guess at intentions, believers and non-believers alike have no difficulty in naming the human agents and pointing to historical reasons for that violent death. However, once we describe the crucifixion as an 'act of God' and maintain the Father's involvement, we step beyond the level of visible history. We not only report what we believe to have been the case at that level of invisible reality, but we also express our personal response. We cannot accept the crucifixion as an 'act of God', without freely committing ourselves. To recognize God's involvement at Calvary is to accept our own involvement there.

A few words of summary should now be in order. We can relate the different agents involved in the execution on Calvary. The activity of Judas, Caiaphas, Pilate and others force us to call it an 'act of man'. God's engagement in the death allows us to name it as an 'act of God'. In the case of Jesus himself, one can speak of an 'act of the God-man'. Viewed one way, he interacted with other human agents. Viewed another way, he was God engaged in our history, revealing his concern for us and finally showing his hand through his violent death. To some major values of that death we turn in our next chapter.

V

THE UNCRUCIFIED IS THE UNHEALED

I have been waiting all my life for someone like you. I knew that someone like you would come and forgive me.

Dostoyevsky, *The Brothers Karamazov*

But reconciled among the stars.

T. S. Eliot, 'Burnt Norton', *Four Quartets*

History never liberates; only man liberates; not history using man as its tool.

Karl Marx, *The Holy Family*

'The martyr is formally described as a hero, but he is more often mourned as a victim.'[1] These words of Raymond Williams strike echoes from the New Testament. One must hasten to add that joy rather than mourning catches more accurately the feelings of the early Christians towards the crucified and risen Jesus. Paul, while steadily recalling the disturbing way his Lord died, nevertheless, saves his tears for his Corinthian converts (II Cor. 2. 4). We never hear that the mother church in Jerusalem built a tomb to recall Christ's *death*, adorned monuments in his honour and wept over the atrocity of his execution.[2] If we put 'mourned' aside, two other words used by Williams ('hero' and 'victim') gather together many characteristic ways the New Testament authors speak of the martyred Jesus. They know him to be mankind's champion as well as mankind's victim.

Thus the book of Revelation impresses us not only with the

victimized Lamb, but also with the blazing beauty of the risen Hero:

> I saw seven golden lampstands, and in the midst of the lampstands one like a son of man, clothed with a long robe and with a golden girdle round his breast; his head and his hair were white as white wool, white as snow; his eyes were like a flame of fire, his feet were like burnished bronze, refined as in a furnace, and his voice was like the sound of many waters; in his right hand he held seven stars, from his mouth issued a sharp two-edged sword, and his face was like the sun shining in full strength. When I saw him, I fell at his feet as though dead. But he laid his right hand upon me, saying, 'Fear not, I am the first and the last, and the living one; I died, and behold I am alive for evermore, and I have the keys of Death and Hades' (1. 12–18).

Hebrews slips from the image of the slaughtered High Priest (chs 5–10) to that of the heroic witness, who battles his way through a shameful death to be enthroned at God's right hand (12. 2).

Looking at the crucifixion, the New Testament writers respond to this 'act of God' with such themes as *power-in-weakness, reconciliation, liberation* and *expiation*. Today none of us can know in advance just how valuable and effective such themes will be in shaping our reaction to Jesus' martyrdom. In handling the scriptural material we can at points help ourselves by recalling his roles as hero and victim. Even so, we may have to be content with modest results. Recognizing value in the crucifixion is not the same thing as being able to give an account of it. This death does not yield up its deeper meaning easily. Its meaning may be constantly disclosed but never finally. disclosed.

Worse than that, the crucifixion affronts our sense of order and meaning. It looks like the extreme case among pointless atrocities, the most disturbing example of meaningless disorder in human affairs. Men conspired to destroy the ultimate Hero. Of course, their action did not prove irreparable. God intervened to raise Jesus from the dead. But this did not relegate the crucifixion to the past, as nothing more than a brutally painful episode which Jesus had to face on his way to resurrection. Paul describes the good news he brings as the message of 'Christ crucified' (I Cor. 1. 23). God made this death by torture killing the focus and source of our values. But the reality of the crucifixion seems to refute all those values we have just cited from the New Testament. A man pinned on a cross symbolizes not power, but the weakness of unspeakable pain. If innocent, his killing adds to human guilt rather than expiating it. What reconciling quality or liberating effects can one detect in such a squalid murder? Should we guess that on Good Friday night Caiaphas and his colleagues slept easily after freeing themselves of the troubles Jesus had generated for them? Luke reports that Herod and Pilate patched up their quarrels 'that very day' (23. 12). One might expect that only such *demonic* liberation and reconciliation could have followed Jesus' death. How could the crucifixion have freed or reconciled anyone else except the villains?

This chapter hunts for ways to clarify the New Testament reaction to the killing of Jesus. We single out for treatment three themes: power-in-weakness, liberation and reconciliation.

Power in Weakness

Paul's theme of 'power-in-weakness' can offer us a way in.[3] The apostle's thought goes beyond some dramatic commonplace about the tragic fall of a prince. The enthusiasm of Palm Sunday peters out, the arrest occurs and the fickle crowd switches to shout for blood. Paul wishes to do more than recall such events and reflect on that fate: 'Yesterday a king, today a crucified criminal.' This would be weakness *following* power, even if – as we shall see – that sequence has its place in the total story. Paul also means utter weakness, not just solitude. Ibsen's character, Stockmann, remarks: 'The strongest man in the world is he who stands most alone.' Mere aloneness fails to match the degrading loss of all human power suffered by the one who 'was crucified in weakness' (II Cor. 13. 4). Who is weaker than a man pinned on a cross to twist in pain and die slowly?

Astonishingly, God acted powerfully to save mankind in and through the ultimate weakness that crucifixion implies. Power and weakness seem mutually exclusive. The last place in the world to look for God's decisive intervention should be Calvary. Left to ourselves, we would nominate the miracles of Jesus, his preaching, or some other exercise of power. He taught with authority, smashed the grip which evil spirits held over their victims (Mark 1. 22, 27), and quickly drew widespread attention to himself. Men murmured their admiration at his success. We might have expected to see him go even further and make one supreme gesture – let us imagine, by recalling an army of the dead back from their graves to outdo even the raising of Lazarus. After that performance, however, his power seemed to slip away. We were to be saved through the weakness of his pain. If contemporaries of Jesus refused to imagine anything good – let alone the expected Messiah – coming out of Nazareth, we can well demand: Can anything good – let alone a redemption powerful enough to save all mankind – come from a crucifixion? But decisive help came precisely from such an unexpected quarter.

Before the cross of its victim evil squatted triumphantly. The crooked line of sin ran through man's history to that confrontation. As Paul puts it, Adam's disobedience opened the road to sin and murder. Men continued to abuse, oppress and hack away at one another, until this sinfulness could and eventually did go as far as murdering the Son of God. The *homo homini lupus* had grown to become *homo Deus-homini lupus*. The sin of Adam came then to its vicious and powerful high-point (Rom. 5. 12ff.). Above the fog of human crime the cross stuck out like a flag run up to celebrate the victory of evil. Jesus looked not only weak but overpowered. The divine 'power-in-weakness' was a force exerting itself in the very place of sin's triumph. God intervened at the point of man's greatest godlessness.

The Pauline theme of 'power in weakness' pushes beyond some such mild-mannered statement as: 'From death comes life.' At the visible level, this death was carried out with the leisurely cruelty of a torture killing. John's agricultural image can blank out the obscene sadism and the unspeakable pain of crucifixion: 'Unless a grain of wheat falls into the earth and dies, it remains alone; but if it dies, it bears much fruit' (12. 24). The soft sense of mother earth beguiles us. It is with slow gentleness and not with abrupt and awful pain that the plant grows from the seed. At the invisible level, man's lust for evil struck Jesus down. He fell into the hands of murderous sin. He did not slip quietly into the arms of sister death. A principle like 'From death comes life' plays down both the agony and the evil. We must insist: 'From murder came life', or 'In crucifixion God gave life'. That was the startling way in which God worked.

The exodus from Egypt had been strange enough. God then formed his special nation out of a group of runaway slaves. But through the crucifixion he created his redeemer out of a murdered man, and his new people out of those who wished to identify with this violent death: 'Do you not know that all of us who have been baptized into Christ Jesus were baptized into his death? We were buried therefore with him by baptism into death' (Rom. 6. 3f.).

Calvary echoes through what the risen Christ has to say to Paul about suffering in the ministry: 'My grace is sufficient for you, for my power is made perfect in weakness' (II Cor. 12. 9). This short sentence (the only words of the risen Lord in Paul's letters) makes us face the crucifixion. God's power was made perfect in his Son's weakness. The risen Christ could have looked back and said about himself: 'When I was weak, then I was strong' (II Cor. 12. 10). But what logic controls the coincidence of power and weakness? None, I suspect, that we can fashion. We simply have to allow that the God who acts in surprising ways outdid himself in making a sordid killing the place where he effectively began to inaugurate his final kingdom. On Calvary the loser was the champion. The victim became the hero. He hung there 'as poor, yet making many rich; as having nothing, and yet possessing everything' (II Cor. 6. 10). We can risk translating this coincidence of power and weakness by parodying an older principle as follows: *the uncrucified is the unhealed*.

Ever since church fathers like St Athanasius hammered it out, the principle 'the unassumed is the unhealed' has enjoyed wide support. According to this principle, unless the incarnate Son of God had assumed every element which belongs to human nature as such, his redemptive grace would not have healed man's life in all its dimensions. We can express the point equivalently by saying: Nothing was healed unless it was assumed.

Can we then take the venerable slogan (which attributes man's redemption to a 'full' incarnation), apply it to the crucifixion, and drastically alter it to read: The uncrucified is the unhealed? Let us note that this formulation goes beyond Paul's explicit sentiments. 'When I am weak, then I am strong' announces only that the two spheres (of weakness and power) coincide. As it stands, his text does not read: 'I am never – or can never be – strong unless I find myself weak.' Likewise the risen Christ does not assure his apostle: 'My power can only be made perfect in weakness', or 'The unafflicted with weakness is the non-perfected with power'. On what basis can we maintain such a necessity and assert that 'the uncrucified is the unhealed'?

Different schools of theologians, no matter how they kicked at one another over the explanation, stood together in holding some 'necessity' for the incarnation. The Word not only became flesh, but – for the reasons given – 'had' to become flesh. For the Scotists, Christ came to bring the world to its appropriate fulfilment – a fulfilment that as a matter of fact entailed healing human sin. Others believed that Christ came only because mankind was lost through sin and needed a heavenly Saviour. Considering the nature of sin and the necessity of satisfaction, St Anselm held that nothing less than the incarnation could provide the means for a solution. Despite their differences, all the theological traditions tried to reconcile the freedom of God's saving love with considerations of reason. They set themselves at some point between two extremes. One pole could so respect the gratuitousness of salvation that the incarnation would look like an arbitrary and mysterious decision on God's part. The other pole could so stress the rational motives for the incarnation that it would appear utterly 'necessary' – in some strong sense of that word.

However we assess the success reached by any of the theories in finding a position between the two extremes, theologians in general showed themselves preoccupied with illustrating a mitigated necessity for the *incarnation*. Frequently they left loopholes for assigning no such firm necessity to the *crucifixion*. It became a commonplace to allow that Jesus could have saved mankind by undergoing any act of suffering – for instance, by submitting to a flogging. Some even suggested that redemption could have come when the infant Jesus was circumcised. He suffered pain and lost a little blood then. There was no need to die atrociously by crucifixion. Those who made the incarnation as such the supreme means of human redemption could readily tolerate – at least in theory – letting the crucifixion go and still having their Christianity whole.

Nevertheless, both Mark 8. 31 and Luke 24. 26 introduce a 'must' when they refer to the passion. They discern a certain necessity in Jesus' death. Neither speaks of a necessary incarnation as such. Paul cites an early Christian creed which also strikes the note of necessity: 'Christ died for our sins in accordance with the scriptures' (I Cor. 15. 3). Those who knew their Old Testament could see that the crucifixion *had* to be. The first Christians discerned in Calvary more than the cruel killing which happened by chance to put a violent end to Jesus' life. They acknowledged that in the divine plan it needed to be so.

We can take up this 'must' *historically* and read it out of the human probabilities of that time. Prophets had frequently been persecuted for fidelity to their mission. So uncompromising a prophet as Jesus would have to pay a heavy price for his obedience to God. Even a moderately astute analyst in first-century Palestine would have reached that conclusion. Human malice made Jesus' suffering and death inevitable.

We can also take up the 'must' (which the early Christians detected in Christ's death), and use it to support our principle, 'the uncrucified is the unhealed'. The principle itself houses two affirmations. (1) Before Jesus could cause our healing, he had to be crucified. His execution prompted the healing. In that sense, if uncrucified, he would not have been our healer. Being 'made perfect' 'through what he suffered', he could 'become the source of eternal salvation to all who obey him' (Heb. 5. 8f.). (2) It was the whole Jesus who was crucified, not – so to speak – just some part of him. Crucifixion destroyed his entire human existence. What remained uncrucified in him would be unhealed in us.

The last chapter suggested that an *implicit soteriology* breaks loose from the words and actions of the historical Jesus. It reaches its full development in the explicit doctrines on salvation presented by Paul and other New Testament authors. Back in the ministry of Jesus itself we can uncover the roots of our principle – whether we take it as 'power in weakness' or 'the uncrucified being the unhealed'. When he was *with* the weak, then he showed himself strong. He searched out the sick, sinful and marginal people of his society. He exploded with power – making their broken bodies whole, bringing pardon to their guilty consciences, and promising them a share in the great party which God would throw at the end of time. The historical Jesus could have remarked, 'When I am with the weak, then I am strong.' He made that point in equivalent terms: 'I came not to call the righteous, but sinners' (Mark 2. 17). Those who believed themselves to be well could not allow the divine physician to exercise his power to cure them. They behaved as if they had made all the winning moves in the competitive game of life. They counted themselves as pious and powerful. In their lives they recognized no crucified areas which called for healing from Jesus.

Jesus never sought to establish a powerful propaganda machine or to set up some efficient organization. He served the weak, seemed uninterested in launching long-range programmes, and invited a set of nobodies to form the core group among his followers. If he preached with power and worked miracles, he remained highly and almost helplessly vulnerable. At the end those intent on killing him had little trouble in rushing him off to execution. Jesus not only stood with weak people, but also could look thoroughly powerless himself. We witness so much promise ruthlessly and tragically cut short, the poignant catastrophe of crucifixion blotting out a glorious life, a ministry full of lost possibilities halted through the disaster of death. Yet Christians experienced and acknowledged God's saving power bursting through the 'weakness' with which Jesus lived and died.

The *beatitudes* yield another glimpse into the shift from an implicit to an explicit soteriology. We can describe the poor, the sorrowful and the persecuted as the weak and the crucified of our world. Jesus looked beyond normal standards to identify them as the truly blessed people. Their poverty, sorrows, tears and persecutions would give way – he promised – to the comfort, joy and laughter of God's kingdom. They would save their lives by losing them. After preaching that message Jesus acted out the beatitudes through his own suffering and death. 'How blest' in fact was he who suffered crucifixion for the cause of right; in the fullest sense the kingdom of heaven was his (Matt. 5. 10). The Sermon on the Mount foreshadowed the death on Calvary. *The crucifixion dramatized the beatitudes*. They had already announced that divine power is made perfect in human weakness.

A slogan summarizes what we have been outlining: *Extra crucem nulla salus* (outside the cross there is no salvation). The healing power of God engages itself most fully in the crucified weakness of man. But the divine gift calls for human commitment. Jesus drew men and women into the events of salvation – both during his ministry and after his resurrection from the dead. The crippled brought their weaknesses to him, sinners came to weep at his feet, repentant racketeers invited him home to celebrate their reconciliation with God. Those who were sick in mind and body allowed themselves to become the ground that bubbled with new life.

When Paul develops his explicit soteriology, he gives fresh force to this element of human involvement. In the second letter to the Corinthians his meditation on the passion merges with a meditation on his own suffering mission. At first he speaks in *more general terms*: 'We are afflicted in every way, but not crushed; perplexed, but not driven to despair; persecuted, but not forsaken; struck down, but not destroyed; always carrying in the body the death of Jesus, so that the life of Jesus may also be manifested in our bodies' (4. 8–10). Then Paul's mood changes, and he lists *specific* 'weaknesses' which grind him down:

> Five times I have received at the hands of the Jews the forty lashes less one. Three times I have been beaten with rods; once I was stoned. Three times I have been shipwrecked; a night and a day I have been adrift at sea; on frequent journeys, in danger from rivers, danger from

robbers, danger from my own people, danger from Gentiles, danger in the city, danger in the wilderness, danger at sea, danger from false brethren; in toil and hardship, through many a sleepless night, in hunger and thirst, often without food, in cold and exposure (11. 24–27).

Of course, the *fact* of Jesus' crucifixion 'in weakness' (II Cor. 13. 4) remains central to Paul's thinking. But the apostle does not fill out the picture by meditating on the arrest, trial, scourging and other items in the passion. Paul's own suffering life supplies *the concrete details*. He recalls the lashings, betrayals and other 'weaknesses' which have afflicted him.

Paul's sufferings spread over a much longer period of time than Jesus' brief ministry and summary execution. Jesus was never stoned, endured scourging only once, and never went through the horror of shipwreck. In sheer quantity and variety the apostle's own passion seems to improve on his master's. Nevertheless, Paul indignantly refuses to allow any comparison between the results of his own sufferings and those of Jesus (I Cor. 1. 13). The crucifixion on Calvary differed from all other episodes of pain and violent death. The divine power coming through that execution could give value to the sufferings of others, not vice versa.

Paul feels drawn into the event of the crucifixion, and lives out in his own subordinate way the truth that God's power will be made perfect in human weakness. Through being victimized Paul becomes the heroic and powerful apostle. Such involvement in the event of Calvary also emerges, when we explore the themes of liberation and reconciliation. It is not finally possible to distinguish between that event and man's response to the event in any absolute way.

Liberation

The first Christians knew that Jesus had 'set them free' through his suffering and death (Gal. 5. 1). He had 'redeemed' them through the event of Calvary (Gal. 3. 13). The book of Revelation praised the Lamb: 'Thou wast slain and by thy blood didst ransom men for God' (5. 9). When E. S. Fiorenza comments on the meaning of 'ransom', she explains:

> The image probably refers here to the slave-market since men are the objects of the purchase. However, it does not advert to the sacral ransom of slaves, where the slave himself had to pay the price under

the fiction that the god, in whose temple he deposited the money, purchased the slave from his human owner, since neither God nor the purchased are paying the price. More probably, the reference is to the ransom of prisoners of war, who were deported to the countries of the victors and who could be ransomed by a 'purchasing agent' of their own country. Here the image refers again to the exodus-tradition. As the blood of the paschal lamb was a sign for the *liberation* of Israel from the bondage and slavery of Egypt, so also is the *liberation* of the Christians from their universal bondage.

No one will fuss very much at the change of image – the ransoming of prisoners of war instead of the manumission of slaves. But the choice of language – 'liberation' as a synonym for 'redemption' – could leave some readers feeling uneasy. Will someone speak of Jesus' self-image as liberator and re-translate Luke 4. 18 accordingly? 'He has sent me to proclaim liberation to the captives and recovering of sight to the blind, to liberate those who are oppressed.' Will such faddish language take over everywhere? Even the 1974 Synod of Bishops in Rome adopted this language in its closing declaration. It spoke of the church's evangelical task to promote 'the true and full *liberation* of all men, groups and peoples' (no. 12; italics mine).

One could try to calm irritation at 'liberation' talk by arguing that this usage has become necessary. Men have defiled the word 'freedom'. An organization intent on murderous violence calls itself 'The Ulster Freedom Fighters'. Corrupt politicians support a neo-colonial war against Asians on the grounds that 'eternal vigilance is the price of freedom'. Men have often corrupted the language of freedom. But 'liberation' has also been defiled by some of the things done or said in its name. Liberation forces may be just as vicious and oppressive as freedom fighters. We cannot fashion our preferences here merely on the basis of use and misuse. The advantage which 'liberation' enjoys over 'freedom' lies elsewhere. It is an 'action word', which implies struggle and vibrates with mobilizing power. The freedom brought by the crucifixion will not keep; it cannot be stored or refrigerated. It remains always in process – something just received, something to be prayed for and worked for. The action initiated by Jesus' death is not yet ended – either on his side (and that of his Father) or on our side. 'Liberation' suggests all that more successfully than 'freedom'.

Granted the choice of language, what kinds of things sound through from our experience, when we count liberation as a

consequence of the crucifixion? Three different sets of examples
suggest themselves: (1) Free people become enslaved but reach
freedom again. (2) Oppressed women are liberated to enjoy equal
rights and opportunities. (3) Children are encouraged to take
responsibility for themselves and become progressively liberated
from parental control. Here we might also think of energy being
liberated, when coal is burnt or atoms are split. Let me illustrate
the cases with a plan.

(1) Free men and women ⟶ slaves ⟶ renewed freedom ⎫
                                                    ⎬ Movement from
                                                    ⎪ evil to good
(2) — ‖ —   — ‖ —   oppressed ⟶ liberation ⎪
                            women   ⎭

(3) — ‖ —   — ‖ —   non-liberated ⟶ liberation ⎫
                            children and   ⎬ Movement from
                            energy   ⎭ good to better

On the one hand, case (1) *differs* from both cases (2) and (3) in
being a three-stage affair. After some captivity men and women
find freedom again but in a new and enhanced form. Their
liberation does not take them back to an earlier stage, but moves
them to a fresh state of renewed freedom. In both cases (2) and (3)
there never was an original, liberated state. Women have been
oppressed from the outset, right from birth children come under
the control of their parents, and energy remains locked within the
coal or atoms until man intervenes. On the other hand, cases (1)
and (2) *resemble* each other in presenting a movement of deliver-
ance, a passage from evil to good. Even though we also speak of
liberation in case (3), it is, however, a passage from good to better
– a movement of growth. When the right time comes, children
should pass a limit and break through into a new state of independent responsibility. We watch a dynamic refusal to settle for
old limitations. Human beings grow into mature adults. Likewise, energy which has been locked up in matter can be released
to serve man's reasonable needs.

The third pair of examples suggest the liberation involved in
the incarnation much more closely than they catch the significance of the crucifixion. Admittedly death touches case (3). When

children grow to maturity, they must let their earlier relationships with their parents change and even shatter. They need to be
willing to die to the old situation before taking up their new
status. The liberation of energy destroys the lumps of coal and the
equilibrium of the atoms. Nevertheless, the primary point of such
examples I take to be the fulfilment of possibilities and a
development to greater completeness. This matches the incarnation more nearly than the crucifixion. When the right time came,
the human race passed a limit and moved into a new state. It
made a decisive leap forward in its upward climb from matter and
multiplicity to spirit and unity. Someone emerged among us,
who spoke with a Galilean accent and looked like other young
Jewish men. But – in an utterly unique sense – this was the Jewish
face of God and the Galilean voice of God. The birth of Jesus
represented an absolute (if unmerited) possibility within human
evolution. It could not be utterly ruled out that, 'when the time
had fully come' (Gal. 4. 4), the Word would take flesh and dwell
among us. Nevertheless, his appearance remains a stunning
development, not a smoothly predictable movement from the
good to the better. A violent atomic explosion rather than the
steady release of energy from a coal-fire hints at the liberating
breakthrough brought by his incarnation.

Cases (1) and (2) reflect more strikingly the *liberation from evil*
effected by the events of Good Friday and Easter Sunday. It has
been a Christian commonplace to link those events with the
achievement of Moses in leading his people from slavery back to
freedom. This comparison can, however, mask a profound difference. On Calvary a crucified victim – not a powerful hero – set
mankind free. It took the dead, not the living, to liberate us. It
took the crucifixion to make a (universal) liberator of Jesus. Here
the new liberation differed astonishingly from its Old Testament
prefigurement. Paul makes his classic plea for Christian freedom
in the letter to the Galatians. This victorious liberation has been
won through the crucifixion! Others were made whole as Jesus
was broken. Nevertheless, he had already inaugurated the process of liberation prior to his death. Once again we observe the
shift from the *implicit* soteriology of the ministry to the *explicit*
soteriology found in the letters of Paul.

In his own person Jesus showed himself devoid of fear, resolutely opposed to evil and totally obedient to his father's will. He
was the truly liberated man, the one freed to be a human being *par
excellence*. Being utterly liberated himself, he could set others free.

His exorcisms delivered men and women from the control of evil powers, his miracles liberated the sick from disease, his pardon called the guilty to the freedom of true creatures. By eating and drinking with sinners, Jesus communicated peace and anticipated the rich happiness to come with the final liberation of God's kingdom. Guilty men and women had been waiting all their lives for someone like him to come and forgive them.

In the post-resurrection situation Paul saw how the crucifixion had in principle smashed the power of sin, and delivered us from the hopeless task of seeking justification through our own performance. Failure to reach prescribed levels of conduct need no longer oppress us. Justification is not something achieved by us, but the grace given to us when we acknowledge our powerlessness and line up with the crucified Jesus (Gal., *passim*). We can now hope to be liberated from death, 'the last enemy' to be overcome so that 'God may be everything to every one' (I Cor. 15. 26, 28). At the same time, however, the gift of liberation entails our commitment: 'For freedom Christ has set us free; stand fast therefore, and do not submit again to a yoke of slavery' (Gal. 5. 1). 'Eternal vigilance', we might say, 'is the price of liberation.' Accepting freedom through the death of Jesus initiates us into a process which will end with the transformation of final resurrection. In that sense there is at present no such thing as being liberated; there is only becoming liberated.

Reconciliation

In providing an account of the results which followed from the crucifixion, Gustav Aulén, Karl Barth and other theologians have made 'reconciliation' one of their favourite words. The theme chosen by Pope Paul VI for the Holy Year of 1975 was reconciliation.[5] Even if the term does not turn up very frequently in the New Testament, it occurs in a particularly prominent way in two sections of Paul's major letters (Rom. 5. 8–11; II Cor. 5. 18–21), as well as in Colossians 1.20 and Ephesians 2. 16. It can look like a respectable and unproblematic notion for expounding the significance of Jesus' death. Nevertheless, reconciliation language resembles that of liberation in presenting not merely one layer of meaning and usage but several. We need to peel away those layers like the skins of an onion – all the time being ready for surprises.[6]

The realms of religious discourse and theological discourse are often characterized by the extraordinary use of ordinary words.

Few places in Christian literature illustrate this situation more clearly than the letters of Paul. The apostle continually tries – sometimes subtly, sometimes with alarming casualness and *naïveté* – to express the message about Christ's death and resurrection in language which, while adequate for ordinary human affairs, remains quite incapable of handling the dealings of God with men. As a result, he is required again and again to force expressions that have their grounding in our world to do substitute service for the unsayable. An inevitable consequence of this situation is that, if we wish to understand Paul rightly, we need to introduce important qualifications into the rules which govern the use of these expressions. We have to do this to the point where we continually hang precariously on the edge of paradox, if not outright contradiction.

Later in this chapter we can examine (1) how Paul employs 'reconciliation' to expound the results of the crucifixion, and (2) see what limitations face us in adopting his expression. But before doing that we need to look first at the use of the term on its home ground in ordinary discourse situations. That may help us to see *both* why this term might be appropriate for our purposes, *and* how far we can accept the consequences of the apostle's usage without landing ourselves in absurdities.

We can characterize theology as the activity of paying attention to the uses of religious discourse. A theologian is not a spokesman for God. It is simply that he watches his language in the presence of God. He is bound by the modest task of getting things straight – a task at times carried out carelessly by writers on the redemption. Gustaf Aulén, for instance, tells us that for him, quite simply, God 'reconciles' the world with himself.[7] A few pages further on he admits to being indifferent 'whether the actual terms used be the forgiveness of sins, union with God, the deifying of human nature, or some other'.[8] To put matters mildly, Aulén runs the risk here of letting his meaning become muddled by inconsistent usage and failure to watch his language. Even with his second preferred term ('set free'), we have noted how we need to sort out our usage there.

As regards the words 'reconcile' and 'reconciliation', there are three main uses which could be relevant to our purposes. We will examine each of them briefly. They have to do, respectively, with (1) the *acceptance* of hard situations or facts; (2) the *removal* of contradictions or incompatibilities; (3) the *removal* of enmity or conflict.

(1) An accident victim may become reconciled to the fact that he will never walk again, or a diabetic may become reconciled to the necessity of taking daily insulin injections. These people have to accept not just ordinary situations, but painful *limitations*. A man does not become reconciled to winning a million dollars in the lottery. The element of struggle needs to be present. A medical student does not become reconciled to discontinuing his studies, if he has not previously struggled against adverse circumstances and failed to overcome them. At the same time, there is also an irreducibly *positive* aura about the use of the term in these situations. Becoming reconciled to the facts is a very different thing from giving up. In short, this first usage of 'reconcile' concerns the positive but difficult acceptance of limitations.

(2) It may be the task of an insurance investigator to reconcile the descriptions of an accident given by several witnesses. A doctor can be asked to reconcile his position on the dangers of cigarette smoking with the fact that he gets through several packets a day. An accountant may reconcile the statement produced by a bank with the different figures shown on some company's books. In all these cases there is a perceived incompatibility which must be resolved, a conflict which must be removed. *There need be no personal conflict* in such situations. In fact, there can be amicable personal relationships, even where differences exist that cannot be reconciled. Two politicians may be close personal friends, in spite of the fact that they hold irreconcilable positions on a number of issues.

(3) A husband and wife can be reconciled after a separation which might have ended in divorce. This is Paul's 'secular' sense of *katallassō* in I Corinthians 7. 11: 'Let her [sc. the wife] be reconciled to her husband.' Two families might be reconciled after years of enmity and dispute. A wayward or headstrong son can be reconciled with his father, after a long period of mutual animosity and rejection. The differences that are reconciled in such situations are often related to those of type two, except that here there exists *personal* involvement on a deep level. Reconciliation in these cases can take place, if (*a*) one party in the dispute admits his error and acknowledges the rightness of the other's position. A son may give up his dissolute life-style and admit that his father's disapproval was justified. Reconciliation can also take place, however, if (*b*) both parties compromise, or even if they come to recognize some higher value which can unite them in spite of continuing to hold tenaciously to deeply-felt but incom-

patible positions. This occurs when the parties agree not to allow their differences to continue to permeate and poison their whole relationship.

It is impossible to be reconciled in this sense with a stranger, or with one to whom I am related only superficially. A man is not reconciled with someone whom he has angered by colliding with him on a crowded pavement. Further, it would be odd to talk of corporations or states being reconciled, because the dimension of personal involvement is lacking in such cases. It would be proper to speak of the reconciliation of the *positions* taken by two nations – for instance, at peace talks. But this is reconciliation in sense (2) above. In cases where such talk of reconciliation seems less odd, the nations in question tend to take on the aspects of families and become personified as social individuals. That is sometimes the case in accounts of the current Arab-Israeli conflict. That would then be sense (3).

A clear presupposition behind this third sense of reconciliation is that (i) there exist some sort of significant personal relationship between the parties involved, and (ii) that there be some sort of real conflict or breach to be resolved. It is in this latter feature that sense (3) of reconciliation enjoys its similarities to the previous two senses. Mere fusion of two different parties is not enough. Some genuine break is required. It is also presupposed that some kind of *interaction* take place between the agents involved; it is not possible that one party to the dispute remain simply passive. A one-sided argument, in which one of the parties refuses to engage the other and shows indifference both to any dispute and its resolution, has no element of real conflict. The resolution can be called reconciliation only in a Pickwickian sense.

What this third sense of reconciliation does *not* presuppose is that the parties to be reconciled necessarily enjoyed an actual relationship of close friendship *prior* to their state of conflict. This may be so. In the examples given above the husband and wife were, presumably, joined in loving intimacy before their separation took place. The estranged families once stood on good terms with each other. The father and his wayward son loved one another before the mutual rejection began. However, what precedes the state of conflict may be simply no personal relationship at all. Two officers who previously did not know each other could join the same army unit and take an instant dislike to one another. Their deep personal animosity might so disrupt the life of the unit that a superior officer could be forced to intervene to settle their differences and so reconcile these warring parties. In such a case, reconciliation would *not* involve the following three stages: (i) that the parties previously stood on terms of close intimacy and friendship; (ii) that a serious breach led to their becoming more or less totally estranged; and (iii) that the good relationship was restored by the conflict being resolved. At most we can speak of the alienated officers finding themselves at first in a context of an *intended relationship* of mutual respect, even if they failed to realize this ideal. Their *actual* relationship passed only through two stages – from an alienation to a reconciliation which nullified the alienation. To mark out such a case we might think of speaking of 'conciliation' rather than 'reconciliation'. But 'conciliation' neither appears to be used anywhere in a theological context, nor stops us from following ordinary usage and talking of reconciliation taking place – *even where stage (i) is absent*. G. D. Kaufman ignores this possibility when he simply assumes that three stages are always involved: 'Reconciliation is the bringing together of parties who had become alienated and reuniting them; relations which had become strained and distorted are brought back to the harmony and peace and fulfilment of friendship and love.'[9] One could cite many further examples of systematic theologians who take it for granted that reconciliation always involves three stages: close friendship, a breach, and the restoration of friendship. The 're' in reconciliation can seduce them into thinking it must always be a three-stage affair.

Before turning to St Paul, we should also note one further feature of reconciliation language. It does *not* necessarily imply that both parties have been guilty of provoking the conflict. Whether we think of quarrels between individuals, feuds between families or conflicts between social individuals like nations, we should cast out any supposition that *both* sides must always be in the wrong.

What has been said so far on 'reconciliation' does not *as such* establish anything about human relationships with God. Our aim has been to illustrate and clarify language – not to allow it to seduce us into snap conclusions about the nature of redemption. For instance, the remarks about the mutual interaction involved in reconciliation should not mislead us into viewing contacts between God and man as an evenly-balanced affair in which both parties play equivalent roles. Likewise none of our examples prove points about redemption. To echo Wittgenstein – they simply remind us to battle against the bewitchment of our theological minds by means of our language.

Let us take up Paul's use of reconciliation. In Romans 5. 8–11 we read:

> But God showed his love for us in that while we were yet sinners Christ died for us. Since, therefore, we are now justified by his blood, much more shall we be saved by him from the wrath of God. For if while we were enemies we were reconciled to God by the death of his Son, much more, now that we are reconciled shall we be saved by his life. Not only so, but we also rejoice in God through our Lord Jesus Christ, through whom we have now received our reconciliation.

II Corinthians 5. 18–20 runs as follows:

> All this is from God, who through Christ reconciled us to himself and gave us the ministry of reconciliation; that is, God was in Christ reconciling the world to himself, not counting their trespasses against them, and entrusting to us the message of reconciliation. So we are ambassadors for Christ, God making his appeal through us. We beseech you on behalf of Christ, be reconciled to God.

Both passages clearly suppose an antecedently-existing enmity between God and man – in which man is the enemy of God. However, the relationship is not symmetrical. If man seems to have viewed God as enemy, God clearly did not see man so. Else he would not have taken the initiative, despite his standing as the aggrieved party in the conflict.

What these passages do *not* presuppose is that man *fell* from an actual situation of friendship with God into one of conflict and hostility. J. A. Fitzmyer finds this sense in Paul's words, when he speaks of 'the *return* of man to God's favor and intimacy after a period of estrangement and rebellion through sin and transgression'.[10] Two stages, however, suffice to account for Paul's language here: (i) a situation of hostility, followed by (ii) a resolution of this conflict and a state of friendship. If we look for a doctrine of the fall, we need to move beyond the apostle's language of reconciliation. Romans 5. 12ff. deals with sin and may deal with so-called original sin. But even such a passage does not necessarily imply a *fall* from an actualized state of original justice and friendship with God.

Our passage from Romans reveals two rather odd aspects in Paul's thought. He pictures human reconciliation with God (*a*) as having already been accomplished, and (*b*) as effected through a third party. As regards (*a*), if this reconciliation has already been accomplished, it seems that human beings need not do anything.

They face a *fait accompli*. As regards (*b*), we must ask how Christ brings about *our* reconciliation with the Father. One can readily understand how reconciliation can come through the good offices of a third party, but it seems clear that the status of this third party must be acknowledged by both sides. If our reconciliation has already been accomplished, however, before we can even acknowledge the role of Christ, in what sense did he represent our interests in this matter?

One might presume that man has shown himself the guilty party in the conflict, he has no interests to represent. But even if that were so, it would still be necessary that man become in some way actively involved in the process of reconciliation. If man continues to be passive while his 'reconciliation' with the Father occurs, indeed if he remains ignorant of the event until *after* Christ's intervention, then 'reconciliation' is here being used in a logically extended sense. Even if Christ enjoys the ontological status of 'universal man' and does not need to be commissioned by mankind as its representative, it would still seem to be necessary that individual men acknowledge in some way Christ's status in order to be reconciled with the Father. The 'reconciliation' which Paul speaks of as having *already* been accomplished, can be reconciliation in potentiality only – or at best inaugurated reconciliation. God has taken the initiative in offering reconciliation and waits upon man's acceptance.

We can contrast a unilateral word like 'save' with 'reconcile' and similar terms concerned with the mutual acceptance of personal relationships. Obviously we can be saved without knowing or willing it. While I am asleep, a highly venomous snake could be poised to strike me. After catching sight of the snake and killing it in time, a friend might decide not to worry me and say nothing about the incident. Objectively he saved me. Subjectively I know nothing of it. Words like 'reconcile', however, imply a mutuality and can be used only improperly of any redemption, so long as it remains merely 'objective'. Of course, an action implying an offer of reconciliation may not be appreciated as such for some time. Nevertheless, in the ordinary sense of the word we cannot be reconciled unless we consciously acknowledge and accept the offer of reconciliation *at the time* that it is made. The recent habit of calling penance 'the sacrament of reconciliation' brings out this dimension of mutual and conscious interaction. It would be less appropriate to describe baptism in this way – at least in those churches which baptize infants.

The parents and godparents help to bring the baby into a new relationship with God, but the baby itself cannot consciously accept the change.

The passage in II Corinthians compounds our problems, since it does not take Christ to be a separate agent at all. The Father emerges as the sole agent in the matter. It is *he* (in Christ) who effects our reconciliation. Once again man remains excluded from active participation. The passage rules out even the concept of vicarious participation through Christ, since it is the Father – not Christ – who takes action. Paul speaks as if reconciliation had already been brought about ('God . . . reconciled us to himself'). Until we have made our move in the transaction, this reconciliation can only turn out to be the offer of reconciliation.

Another problem should be mentioned. At the end of the passage from II Corinthians, Paul pleads with his audience to 'be reconciled with God'. This almost sounds as if God were the guilty party and man (as the aggrieved party) has to forgive God. I think, however, that the reconciliation spoken of here corresponds – at least partially – to our sense (1) above. God has saved mankind, and man should be reconciled to this fact and order his life accordingly. If reconciliation is simply meant in sense (3), then an incompatibility emerges between this verse and those which suggest that the reconciliation has *already* taken place.

We should allow for two further problems, as we watch our language about reconciliation. The first arises from the New Testament itself, and the second from contemporary Western society. Colossians 1. 20 announces that through Christ God chose 'to reconcile to himself all things, whether on earth or in heaven'. Ernst Käsemann has detected here a primitive *cosmological* sense of reconciliation, which the author of the epistle later turned in an anthropological direction. On this view 'reconciliation' meant – at least at the earliest stage of Christian discourse – a cosmic transference of dominion which resulted in cosmic peace. Even if the anthropological sense historically preceded the cosmological, such cosmic reconciliation would still seem odd. Given that reconciliation occurs between *moral agents* who reach agreement after conflict, in what sense can God choose to reconcile to himself a hostile cosmos and – what is more – do this unilaterally? The passage may, however, act as one more reminder that Western Christians have lost their feeling for the interconnectedness of all things. Sin has hurt nature and left it estranged from God. Man and the cosmos make up a kind of 'mythical collective', in which the human beings can stand in conscious alienation from God. They can not only become aware of what sin does to such a mythical collective, but also experience this cosmos being reconciled to God.

Our second problem concerns the danger of 'reconciliation' becoming devalued. Interested parties with privileges to defend in society or church smile pleasantly and use this word. But too often the terms of reconciliation which political and ecclesiastical leaders have in mind turn to their own advantage. They prefer to suppress conflict, in order to preserve their power. Weaker parties – even if they are not blatantly exploited and deprived – will have none of this. They prefer to demand justice and liberation rather than nod agreement to calls for reconciliation. One can only hope that it is not indulging theological melodramatics to express a wish here. It might be a way to heal some wounds in society and church, if the masters – or at least the stronger parties – adopted the language of liberation, while the victims – or at least the weaker parties – took up reconciliation talk.

Here, of course, we touch the theme of involvement which has already emerged in the discussion of liberation and power-in-weakness. Reconciliation is not over and done with when God and mankind become reconciled through Christ. The gift of reconciliation draws human beings into reconciling action. It is not finally possible to distinguish in any absolute way between *the* reconciliation effected through Christ, and man's response to that event expressed in many reconciliations. St Paul sees the great opportunity for such reconciliations in the altered relationship between Jews and Gentiles. Today we do not have to look far to add other fields for the work of reconciliation: conflict among races, the opposition between the capitalist and Communist worlds, the oppression of developing countries by neo-colonial powers, and the wounded relationship between men and women almost everywhere.

Conclusion

The kind of theology found in this chapter may have put a considerable strain on the reader's interpretative and sympathetic energies. At this point it could help to draw matters together.

First, anyone who reflects on the consequences of Jesus' death needs to get things straight and sort out the usage of 'power-in-weakness', 'liberation', 'reconciliation' or whatever other terms are employed. Merely rehearsing their biblical origins may be no more than a way of concealing our theology's soft centre from scrutiny. The reader should not be kept short of information about the use, misuse and limits of redemption language. None of the terms and images can adequately conceptualize what came about through the death of Jesus. But cumulatively they can perform a helpful descriptive function. This holds true for his titles: Son of God, Son of Man, Saviour, Messiah, Suffering Servant and the rest. None of these many titles fully identifies and describes the person of Jesus. Likewise neither 'reconciler' nor 'liberator' nor any other term describes adequately the redemptive work of Jesus. We need to watch our language and its limitations in the presence of God.

The language of soteriology, however, has often fallen into careless hands. Christology is different. The early controversies about the identity of Christ turned on vast debates about terms like *homoousios, homoiousios, hypostasis, physis, natura, prosopon* and *substantia*. These debates helped to sensitize the Christian church as a whole to its language about the *person* of Christ. The *work* of Christ has never faced such long and widespread controversies and reflection. Sloppy talk in soteriology is understandable, if not excusable.

Second, no matter what terms we prefer, our doctrine of salvation should draw two basic distinctions between (1) the implicit soteriology of Jesus' ministry and the explicit soteriology of the early church, and (2) the events of Good Friday and Easter Sunday themselves and the involvement which they evoke. No one can recognize in the death and resurrection of Jesus the focus and source of his values, without being drawn into this drama.

Two questions need to be treated, if this book on the crucifixion is not to remain patently incomplete. How can we find real sense in the frequent New Testament claim that Christ's death made amends for human sin? Whether we understand the crucifixion as atoning, liberating, reconciling or doing anything else, what account can we give of the *universal* value that Christians detected in that victimization which he accepted? Christ did not die for some others, but 'for all' (II Cor. 5. 14).

VI

ATONEMENT FOR ALL

An almost exclusive reliance upon the limited teaching of the Fourth Gospel in respect of the death of Christ is in no small degree responsible for the widespread, but rapidly disintegrating conviction that we have said all that is important about the atonement when we declare that Christ died in order to embody and make known the love of God for men.

Vincent Taylor, *The Atonement in New Testament Teaching*

You say that it [sc. the death of Christ] appeased His [sc. God's] wrath. I am not sure there may not be some meaning of those words which does not include the truth which they try to express, but in the natural sense which men gather from them out of their ordinary human uses, I do not believe that they are true.

Phillips Brooks, *Sermons* (7th series)

With easy assurance St Paul tosses off his belief that the crucifixion made amends for all human sin: 'Christ died for the ungodly' (Rom. 5. 6) – one man 'dying for all' (II Cor. 5. 14). Once we agree to examine this belief, however, we may find ourselves squirming under the problems it raises.

How could *one* event in history carry such *universal* implications? It seems puzzling that the passion and violent death which swept Jesus away within a few hours could – both retrospectively as well as prospectively – atone for the mass of evil which men and women have committed and will commit through all the centuries. In any case it looks an outrage to our notions of what is just and right to make such a connection between human suffering and the expiation of human sin.

The undeserved death of an utterly righteous man suggests an enormous injustice that adds to human guilt rather than an event which alone would cleanse a rotten world. If we maintain that the crucifixion made reparation for mankind's sin, what else are we doing than subsuming this event under dubious principles? The concept of retributive justice has been deeply eroded even on the purely human scene. Criminals should be cured by appropriate treatment, or – where that may be impossible – at least deterred from damaging society by the threat of formidable punishment. Talk about paying a penalty for their crimes needs to be unmasked. Is this only an oblique expression of society's desire to take vengeance on them? Do we dare to take such a disreputable notion, insert it into the field of human-divine relations, and expound the death of Jesus as the chief or even the indispensable way mankind made retribution for its sins? It has become a commonplace to deny any form of retributive justice. Talk of expiating guilt through suffering has been so long discredited, that it hardly seems worth exhuming and beating this particular dead horse.

In his *Religio Medici* Sir Thomas Browne wrote: 'There are, as in Philosophy, so in Divinity, sturdy doubts and boisterous objections, wherewith the unhappiness of our knowledge too neerely acquainteth us.' I do not wish to line up a few half-hearted objections and then become beastly to these straw men. Any serious reflection can only stir 'sturdy doubts and boisterous objections' against understanding the crucifixion to make atonement for all. Before examining this interpretation, however, it may be as well to clear away first one common and deadly piece of nonsense. Making 'atonement', offering 'reparation', performing some work of 'satisfaction', 'expiating' sin or whatever similar term we wish to use does *not* coincide with 'propitiating' an angry God bent on 'punishing' his Son for the sins of the human race.

Propitiation and Punishment

To prevent matters from turning confused and confusing, we need to note the distinction between propitiation and punishment. (1) Propitiation refers to human action towards God. Man is thought to change the divine mind, and so render an angry deity favourable or at least willing to forgive. (2) In our context punishment covers God's action in chastising sinful man. He could punish out of love, and *need not* be spoken of as angry.

Further, God may be understood to punish someone not as an individual but as a substitute for others In that case one speaks of penal substitution. Propitiation and punishment, although distinct notions, are often blended together by given theories of redemption. 'The unhappiness of our knowledge too neerely acquainteth us' with the tortured ways theologians have combined these two ideas, once St Anselm (*c*. 1033–1109) became the first Christian writer to devote a treatise explicitly to the atonement.

In his *Cur Deus Homo* Anselm maintained that, where human sin offends the divine honour, either 'satisfaction, or punishment must follow every sin'.[1] By making satisfaction, Christ as a matter of fact restored God's honour. Punishment was not imposed. Later writers, however, insisted on choosing this alternative rejected by Anselm.

Punitive elements turned up in the accounts of redemption offered by Alexander of Hales (*c*. 1186–1245), St Thomas Aquinas (*c*. 1225–1274) and other medieval theologians. This development reached a ferocious peak with John Calvin (1509–64), the apostle of God's anger. In Calvin's view Jesus became the personal object of divine reprobation. Through the passion he suffered an abandonment by God that corresponded to the lot of those condemned to hell. This suffering as a penal substitute rendered God favourable and turned away the divine anger. Calvin explained matters thus:

> Christ . . . has taken upon himself and suffered the punishment which by the righteous judgment of God impended over all sinners . . . by this expiation God the Father has been satisfied and . . . his wrath appeased.[2]

Roman Catholic writers showed no pre-ecumenical scruples about echoing this language. Thus J. B. Bossuet (1627–1704), one of the great preachers of all time, described as follows Christ's sufferings:

> The man, Jesus Christ, has been thrown under the multiple and redoubled blows of divine vengeance . . . As it vented itself, so his [God's] anger diminished; he struck his innocent Son as he wrestled with the wrath of God . . . When an avenging God waged war upon his Son, the mystery of our peace was accomplished.[3]

Bossuet credited the Virgin Mary with appropriate sentiments on Calvary:

> She dreams not of asking the Eternal Father to lessen her anguish by

one single throb, when she beholds Him pouring out the full vials of His wrath on the head of His Only-begotten.[4]

On both sides of the denominational divide between Catholics and Protestants this language of propitiation and punishment has flourished down to our own day. Preachers, theologians and hymn-writers continued to represent the suffering Christ as either rendering an angry Father favourable to mankind, or being punished in place of sinful men and women. Even Karl Barth (1886–1968), one of the two or three greatest theologians of this century, endorsed the penal substitution view. Jesus Christ, the man-for-other-men, entered the heart of their alienation from God, took the place of those judged by the divine justice and became himself the object of God's anger. On Golgotha he carried man's sin and culpability, for which he was condemned and punished by death. 'He stands', Barth wrote, 'before the Father at Golgotha burdened with all the actual sin and guilt of man and of each individual man, and is treated in accordance with the deserts of man as the transgressor of the divine command.'[5]

We can parody some words of Dietrich Bonhoeffer to describe this whole tradition of propitiatory and penal theories of redemption. Shortly before he died Bonhoeffer wrote: 'Only the suffering God can help . . . that is the reversal of what the religious man expects from God.'[6] So many religious men seem to have expected that only an angry God can save and only a punishing God can help!

Of course, views built around propitiation and punishment did incorporate several important and persuasive themes. These views strongly pressed the seriousness of human culpability. Sin could cause God to strike down even his own Son, the substitute for his guilty brothers and sisters. Nothing short of Calvary could appease the divine anger at human sin. By way of contrast, some contemporary views of the redemption can let the vicious face of evil slip out of the picture – particularly those views which stress the example of faith and love given by Jesus. His life and death become little more than exemplary events which challenge us to generosity. We are asked to admire this ideal of moral perfection, but not to recall the ugly malice of man's sin. Such an ethical approach does not really tackle and resolve pressing questions of guilt. Let Gabriel Moran serve to illustrate this approach.

An exemplification of faith and a realization of love, . . . the life of Jesus created a new way of life among those who found his teaching and example to resonate in their lives. Even among the enemies of Christianity the ideal of the Christ figure has not found adequate substitute . . . Jesus of Nazareth was one of the supreme individuals who tried to show with his life that the affirmation of the individual is not in negation of the community.[7]

Views that focus on the example of love and faith given by Jesus can be soft on evil. But one could never accuse theologies of propitiation and punishment of failing to take sin seriously. They indicate the hideousness of moral evil by stressing what it cost Jesus to make amends. The atonement meant bearing all human malice and being crushed by the divine anger. Such theologies have here a second 'advantage'. God ceases to be an unchanged bystander, a feudal overlord watching it all impassively from the sky. He becomes emotionally involved, open to change and no longer a cold spectator of the human scene. (In parenthesis, we can note how the same yearning for a God who is involved serves to support process theology, even if that school of theology has so far failed to produce a satisfactory christology and soteriology. The recent flight to process theology expresses the dissatisfaction many people feel at classical views, which represent God as unchanged by man's activity.)

Propitiation and punishment versions of redemption fail, however, on two major scores: their monstrous view of God and their misuse of the New Testament. It seems atrocious to picture anyone – let alone God the Father himself – with extreme cruelty treating someone as a sinner, who is known to be utterly innocent. Yet Calvin, Bossuet and their latter-day followers can tolerate such an image of God as an angry punisher. J. L. McKenzie remarked once: 'A people who are vindictive – and just about everybody is – expect their god to be vindictive.' Maybe. In any case, 'vindictive' – as we shall see – is a risky and ambiguous word in the context of redemption. We need to reflect a little more closely on the human factors that continue to dictate a savage image of God.

Gregory Baum lays his finger on two elements that lurk behind the image of God as an angry punisher: the pathology of the institution, and personal pathology. A punishing God has obviously helped to justify and protect institutional authority, both secular and ecclesiastical. This is not to allege that rulers and church superiors consciously fostered such an image of God as a prop for their position. The image resulted naturally enough from the way they (and their subjects) experienced and interpreted human authority. Fear of God was mobilized in the service of subjection to earthly bosses. At the personal level, 'the idea of God as judge on a throne, meting out punishment, corresponds to a self-destructive trend of the human psyche'.[8] Drives to self-punishment, the anxiety to propitiate forces within oneself and crippling worries about the evil consequences of one's action – all of these elements can coalesce to project a God made in their image and likeness.

Propitiation and punishment theologies of redemption normally latch on to a few New Testament texts like II Corinthians 5. 21, Romans 8. 3 and – particularly – Galatians 3. 13. But none of these passages provides the required backing. The text from Galatians reads: 'Christ redeemed us from the curse of the law, having become a curse for us – for it is written, "Cursed be every one who hangs on a tree".' In dying like a legal criminal according to the definition of Deuteronomy 21. 22f., Jesus saved us – paradoxically – from the curse which the regime of that law entailed. The text of Deuteronomy runs as follows: 'And if a man has committed a crime punishable by death and is put to death and you hang him on a tree, his body shall not remain all night upon the tree, but you shall bury him the same day, for *a hanged man is accursed by God*.' Paul has carefully removed the words 'by God', when he quotes Deuteronomy. It was *not* God but those administering the law who treated Jesus as a criminal worthy of death.

The final verse from II Corinthians 5 is as follows: 'For our sake he [sc. God] made him [sc. Christ] to be sin who knew no sin, so that in him we might become the righteousness of God.' We can unpack the point of Paul's dense text in various ways: (1) 'Christ came in a humanity like that of sinners – except for his being innocent of sin'; or (2) 'God sent the sinless Christ into a sinful world'; 'Christ came as a victim for sin, a sin-offering on our behalf, although he was innocent of sin'; or (3) 'Although being innocent of sin, Christ submitted to the regime of the law which was the regime of sin'. It takes strong dogmatic pre-conceptions to push the passage toward this conclusion: 'God piled the full weight of human sin upon the innocent Christ, condemned him and punished him with death. In brief, God treated the sinless Christ as if he were a sinner.'

Lastly, Romans 8. 3 fails to support propitiation and punishment accounts of the redemption: 'God has done what the law, weakened by the flesh, could not do: sending his own Son in the likeness of sinful flesh and (*a*) for sin, (*b*) he condemned sin in the flesh.' The two segments (*a*) and (*b*) call for brief comment. The New English Bible suggests alternative paraphrases of the cryptic 'for sin': 'as a sacrifice for sin', or 'to deal with sin and take away sin'. As for (*b*), defenders of the penal substitution view insist on taking it to mean, 'God in his anger passed judgment against a *sinner* (his Son, who bore all man's guilt by means of the human nature he had assumed), and condemned him to death'.

Paul maintains that the divine judgment was passed *against sin*, not against Christ (nor – for that matter – against sinful men and women). Besides, could we ever explain how the culpability for personal sins was transferred from those who actually committed them to another person, the innocent Christ? It seems absurd to hold that this guiltless man could literally carry the moral guilt of others. In fact Paul does not defend such nonsense. We can unpack his text as follows: 'God sent his own Son to deal with sin by undergoing the sign and consequence of sin, death. The Son died innocent of sin, but "in a form like that of our own sinful nature" (NEB). Through that death God condemned and triumphed over sin by making the means of sin (the flesh) the means of victory.'[9]

As we have noted, the theme of God's *anger* forms an essential part of a propitiation theory and may also belong to punishment versions of the redemption. Here such propitiation and punishment theologies seem to enjoy stronger biblical backing than when they misuse a few isolated texts from Paul. If we marshal the findings of scriptural scholarship, we cannot allege that the New Testament celebrates only the divine love and drops the Old Testament theme of divine anger. This theme surfaces in the synoptic gospels, John, Paul and elsewhere in the New Testament.[10] Gustav Stählin rehearses the evidence and draws the conclusion: the two testaments may not be contrasted on the basis of a facile distinction between anger and love.

> In the New Testament, then, the wrath of God is in no sense regarded as an inconsistent bit of Old Testament religion which has been dragged in, as though reference to God's wrath belonged only to the Old Testament and reference to His love were confined to the New Testament. For the Old Testament, too, proclaims God's love and mercy just as impressively as His wrath, and the New Testament preaches His wrath as well as His mercy.[11]

We need to deal with possible misrepresentations here. the divine anger expresses God's incompatibility with sin. God stands radically against moral evil and could never be its accomplice. One day this opposition between wickedness and divine integrity will be made manifest. Paul can warn the sinners: 'By your hard and impenitent heart you are storing up wrath for yourself on the day of wrath when god's righteous judgment will be revealed' (Rom. 2. 5). In a special way the apostle links the divine anger with the judgment to come at the end. But *neither Paul nor anyone else in the New Testament connects God's anger with the passion and death of Jesus*. We should press this point strongly. The evangelists, Paul and other New Testament writers both (1) introduce the theme of divine anger, and (2) recall the crucifixion of Jesus. But no one ever uses the notion of divine anger to explain Calvary.

Atonement

Once we have cleared away any talk of propitiation and punishment, we can turn to examine the New Testament belief that through his death Jesus made amends for mankind's sin. This belief houses two convictions: (1) Jesus suffered to atone for sinners (Rom. 5. 6); (2) this suffering was 'according to the scriptures' and in some sense necessary (I Cor. 15. 3; Mark 8. 31). We bump up against immense difficulties here which go beyond merely questioning (2): What kind of necessity – in any sense of 'necessity' – can we detect in Jesus having suffered to make amends for our malice? In proposing *even* non-necessary retributive suffering, we seem to be reviving a notion that has been discredited in modern times and in any case long ago superseded by the New Testament.

Let me introduce a diagram which can serve to illustrate the issues.

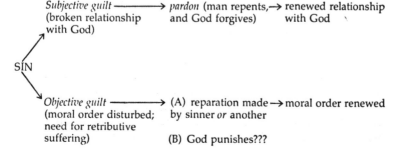

Granted that sin has been truly committed and subjective guilt incurred, surely we should not look for anything more than that the sinner should repent and be forgiven? An autonomous moral law cannot forgive him. But a personal agent (God) can. Once the sinner goes beyond mere regret to genuine repentance, we need not demand anything further from him. God's mercy will be there to renew his life of grace. The steps outlined on the *top* line of the diagram seem both required and sufficient. Even in merely human affairs it has become hard enough to maintain the principle of objective guilt. By no means everyone admits that true responsibility entails that men should accept the consequences of their actions and pay any penalties which they may have incurred. If all agreed, however, that the equivalent of the *bottom* line applied to relationships between man and man, can we apply it to the man–God relationship? The nature of divine mercy and love appears to rule out any need for such reparation. Insistence on reparation would give (retributive) justice an unacceptable priority over this mercy and love. Alternative (B) would make matters worse by bringing us back to the ugly notion of a punishing God.

One should not, of course, create extra difficulties here. We are not talking about suffering in general, but only about retributive suffering. Two issues present themselves: Does such retributive suffering make sense when we deal with human offences against God? Can someone else (the innocent Jesus) assume – representatively – this retributive suffering on behalf of his brothers and sisters? Subjective guilt remains personal and untransferable. But can another human being step in to make reparation for our objective guilt? Admittedly human society could allow someone to pay a fine for me after I have been found guilty of some offence. Some societies might even allow another to go to gaol in my place. But surely we would expect that God, who recognizes that human sin has more the character of disease than crime, would remit the penalty for wrongdoing and concentrate on reclaiming us to live as true creatures?

By this time some readers may feel that at least caution suggests that it might be better not to ask more of these questions, since satisfactory answers are unlikely to be found. Others will suspect that even by themselves such questions suffice to render implausible the belief that Jesus atoned for human sin through his suffering. All in all, however, questions about atonement confront us with the task of clarifying our primordial moral insights – not with the impossible task of attempting to find hard proof for them. It may be best to come clean with my own convictions, and add some reflections that could help to recommend them.

(1) Through his suffering and death Jesus made amends for the objective guilt of human sin, thus restoring and renewing a disrupted moral order. (2) His passion should not be construed as punishment. Loving obedience led him to undertake this act of reparation in solidarity with his brothers and sisters. (3) We must not introduce 'cosmic calculations' by assessing, as it were, the amount of reparation owed. It would be a bizarre procedure to reckon quantitatively, as though one were dealing with some huge gaol sentence incurred by the human race.

(4) The atonement made by Jesus in no way exempts sinners from the need to repent, seek divine forgiveness and enter a new relationship with God. In our diagram the top line remains primary. Reparation has at best a subordinate place. (5) The innocent Jesus unilaterally offered reparation for others. But sinful men and women need to ratify this deed by accepting with gratitude the fact that he made amends on their behalf.

The Old Testament can help us to acquire insight here – as Barth realized. Unlike Anselm, Aulén, Bultmann and many other theologians of the redemption, he took the history of Israel – despite its size – as the proper context for interpreting the crucifixion. Those who have a taste for small points and small steps will probably not like what follows. They will have a sense of important things whizzing by at a breathless rate. But dwelling too long on detail would thwart the purpose of testing our basic convictions on two issues: retributive suffering and the possibility of its being undertaken representatively.

In general the Old Testament speaks more of a national and collective guilt than of personal guilt. Jeremiah and Ezekiel take issue with a traditional proverb when insisting on the individual nature of responsibility and retribution.

> The word of the Lord came to me again: 'What do you mean by repeating this proverb concerning the land of Israel, "The fathers have eaten sour grapes, and the children's teeth are set on edge"? As I live, says the Lord God, this proverb shall no more be used by you in Israel. Behold, all souls are mine; the soul of the father as well as the soul of the son is mine: the soul that sins shall die' (Ezek. 18. 1–4; cf. Jer. 31. 29ff.).

Whether the Old Testament treats of guilt collectively or personally, it may view each guilt not only *subjectively* (our top line) but also see it as an *objective* defilement to be expiated, a debt to be paid, or a punishment to be imposeu (our bottom line). The Israelites cherished one long-standing conviction, the law of equivalence. If every act of faithfulness could expect its due reward, every transgression must receive its just retribution. At times this law assumed the form of an inexorable principle of savagely exact retribution. At other times the law of equivalence expressed itself in vaguer forms of retributive justice.

The story of David's sin highlights the place of reparation (II Sam. 11. 2–12. 25). Nathan stirs the king to repentance after he has committed adultery with Bathsheba and then engineered the death of Uriah, the injured husband. When David confesses, 'I have sinned against the Lord', Nathan assures him: 'The Lord has put away your sin.' The story meets the requirements of the top line in our diagram. Nevertheless, David must also make amends. The child born of his affair dies to expiate 'objectively' the royal sin. This identification of a baby's death as retributive suffering reflects a primitive (and for many people distasteful) mentality. We bump up against belief in a God who punishes – 'visiting the iniquity of the fathers upon the children' (Ex. 20. 5). Israelite history may also leave us puzzled and even disquieted by a liturgical institution designed to offer reparation for sin –Yom Kippur or the Day of Atonement.

The Babylonian exile gave a greater prominence both to sin and rites of expiation to be performed either for oneself or for others. On the Day of Atonement the Israelites aimed to make amends for their offences, purify their guilt and renew their fellowship with God. The people fasted, the high-priest offered various animals, and their blood sprinkled on the covering of the ark (which represented the divine presence) was understood to restore communion with God. As part of the ceremony, the guilt of the people was symbolically transferred to the so-called scapegoat, which was *not* killed but driven away into the desert as unclean.

> Aaron shall lay both his hands upon the head of the live goat, and confess over him all the iniquities of the people of Israel, and all their transgressions, all their sins; and he shall put them upon the head of the goat, and send him away into the wilderness by the hand of a man who is in readiness. The goat shall bear all their iniquities upon him to a solitary land, and he shall let the goat go in the wilderness (Lev. 16. 21f.).

On the one hand, it may be a relief to remind ourselves that the

New Testament nowhere sees the scapegoat as prefiguring the atonement made by Jesus. If he died 'outside the gate' (Heb. 13. 12), neither the letter to the Hebrews nor any other New Testament book portrays Jesus as being contaminated with guilt, driven like the scapegoat out of 'the camp' (Heb. 13. 13) and then – unlike the original scapegoat – being killed there. On the other hand, the transferral of guilt to the goat makes culpability look like a 'thing', which can be detached from responsible moral agents and attached to a creature lacking the power of intelligent freedom. The use of the scapegoat can leave us with the uncomfortable question: Will the notion of retributive suffering for another always entail such a mechanistic procedure?

Before concluding this rapid look at the Old Testament, we need to recall two further developments in thinking about the atonement: the Servant of the Lord oracles found in Isaiah (52. 13–53. 12) and the Maccabean doctrine on martyrdom. Both the excessive sufferings of the Israelites and their heightened consciousness of sin lay behind the picture of the one who 'was wounded for our transgressions and bruised for our iniquities' (53. 5). This suffering Servant of the Lord could stand for an individual, a faithful remnant, the nation itself, or even both an individual and a corporate figure at the same time. Whether understood individually or collectively, the image of the Servant offered some insight into the sufferings which continued to flay not only the people as a whole but also the holiest among them. This Servant atoned representatively for the sins of others. He suffered and died on their behalf.

The Servant of the Lord oracles do not go as far as to endorse the kind of necessity we will find in the letter to the Hebrews. That New Testament book holds (1) that 'without the shedding of blood there is no forgiveness of sins' (9. 22), and (2) that the sacrifice of animals cannot serve to expiate guilt. 'It is impossible', we read, 'that the blood of bulls and goats should take away sins' (10. 4). Isaiah 53 proposes a more modest doctrine: the Servant's death as a matter of fact served to made amends 'for the transgressors' (v. 12). In that way the suffering destiny of the one benefited the many. Mark 10. 45 echoes this sentiment: 'The Son of man also came not to be served but to serve, and to give his life as a ransom for many.'[12]

The lurid martyrdoms of the Maccabean period evoked similar convictions. Through their sufferings and death these righteous martyrs atoned for the sins of their guilty people. Eleazar prayed:

'Make my blood their purification, and take my life to ransom their lives' (IV Macc. 6. 29). The solidarity of such martyrs with the Israelites allowed them to heal and help the sinful community: 'Through them . . . our country was purified, they having as it were become a ransom for the nation's sin' (IV Macc. 17. 20–22).[13] This sentiment from IV Maccabees anticipates the letter to Titus, which acknowledges a similar atoning value in the martyrdom of Jesus: 'Christ . . . gave himself for us to redeem us from all iniquity and to purify for himself a people of his own who are zealous for good deeds' (2. 13f.).

To sum up. Pre-Christian Judaism maintained not only the function of retributive suffering in making amends for sin, but also recognized that the innocent Servant (Isa. 53) or the righteous martyrs (the books of Maccabees) could make such amends representatively. The suffering endured on behalf of others restored and renewed the moral order. These beliefs surfaced in the pastoral letters, Paul's authentic letters, the gospels and elsewhere in the New Testament. But were such inherited convictions no more than superseded structures which the first Christians took time to dismantle – deviations which continued to offer emotional resistance to the good news brought by Jesus Christ? Should retributive suffering – either for oneself or for another – keep any place in a Christian understanding of salvation? Such a doctrine appears to set limits to the divine mercy and deny the generous forgiveness which the prodigal son story exemplifies (Luke 15. 11–32).

Nevertheless, we are not dealing with some minor doctrine of the Old Testament which here and there filtered down like watered wine. The belief that Christ died for our sins is perpetually vivid in the New Testament from later books like the pastorals right back to the early formulations that Paul quotes. 'I delivered to you', he assures his Corinthian converts, 'what I also received, that Christ died for our sins' (I Cor. 15. 3). In his passion Jesus represented us and made atonement for our guilt, which had disrupted the moral order of the universe. During his preaching he had not denied the (subordinate) place of retributive suffering in man's return from sin. What if the prodigal son had calculated the rate at which his friends and money were running out, and avoided hunger and humiliation by going home earlier? The father's merciful love would presumably have expressed itself in the same way, but the parable would leave us feeling uncomfortable. It would lack the element of suffering, which is secondary but integral. In the actual story the boy accepts as his due the afflictions which come to him as a consequence of his wrong-doing. This suffering brings him to repentance, helps to purify him from guilt and – one can say – sets him in renewed harmony with the objective reality of the moral order. The prodigal son makes amends for his sins, enters a new relationship with the moral order, and begins a fresh life of enhanced love in his father's home.

All in all, it does not seem possible to deduce the biblical theme of atonement from some prior principle, or to subsume it under some other doctrine which could be established independently. We are dealing with a primary insight. Much of the routine polemic against atonement, however, has arisen, I suspect, in reaction to the ways this theme has been misrepresented or even viciously misused. Let me summarize some of the major difficulties under three headings: God, Christ and ourselves.

The Case against Atonement

(1) God misrepresented

Misleading accounts of God can run two ways. On the one hand, the *opponents* of atonement risk adopting a highly voluntarist version, in which God grants man a cheap forgiveness that scarcely differs from condoning human evil. In such a version of the aftermath of sin, God seems to lack fidelity towards the universe which he has created, and its moral order which has been disrupted. Like a sponge, man's surroundings absorb the evil effects of his malice. Shakespeare's *Macbeth* demonstrates how man's potential for evil can flower into act to harm and destroy his environment. Few plays illustrate so vividly the way sin violates and disturbs our world. Neither his wife nor the witches force Macbeth to commit his horrible crimes. He never denies his responsibility for what he has done in sinning and ravaging his country. Let us take this case back to our diagram. In discussing the possible conversion of the Macbeths of our world, the opponents of atonement attend only to the top line and dismiss the bottom line. When showing mercy to sinners even worse than Macbeth, God can ignore the need to set right a sin-charged environment, or at best can restore it himself by a simple *fiat* of the divine will.

On the other hand, the supporters of atonement can slip over into talking of God as a punisher, even a vindictive punisher. Our diagram indicates two possible ways of restoring a moral order disturbed by objective guilt: (A) retributive suffering freely undertaken for onself or another, and (B) punishment imposed by God. To be sure, the Old Testament can not only slip from (A) to (B) in speaking of remedies for human sin, but also attribute the punishment to divine anger. One can instance the martyrdom of the mother and her seven sons in II Maccabees. When King Antiochus was about to torture and kill the youngest son, the boy proclaimed his belief:

> I, like my brothers, give up body and life for the laws of our fathers, appealing to God to show mercy soon to our nation and by afflictions and plagues to make you confess that he alone is God, and through me and my brothers to bring to an end *the wrath of the Almighty which has justly fallen on our whole nation* (II Macc. 7. 37f.).

At this point a healthy Christian doctrine of atonement needs to dissociate itself partly from its Jewish background. It agrees with the Old Testament on the role of retributive suffering, but insists that this did not take the form of Jesus enduring retributive punishment for others.

Hence belief in the atonement made by Christ does not as such mean endorsing a place for retributive justice when human society faces crime in its midst. Here retributive justice means retributive punishment. Society not only wishes to deter potential criminals and reform actual ones, but also insists that law-breakers must pay an appropriate penalty. Support for such retributive punishment may, of course, prove a fairly thin veil through which the naked desire for revenge is frequently visible. But whether the appeal to retributive justice in handling crime *always* cloaks vicious vindictiveness can be left aside. Personally I want to part company with those who hold this postition. However, as such the question is irrelevant in our context. The atonement made by Christ consisted of suffering freely undergone, not a ferocious punishment imposed on him as a substitute for guilty humanity.

(2) Christ misrepresented

Two perspectives which organize the material about Christ's work of atonement can get out of focus: his solidarity with us and his sacrifice for us. In the last part of this chapter we will return to his solidarity. Here let me insist simply that it takes the form of his being a *representative rather than a substitute*. For X to act as substitute for Y less intentionality may be needed on both sides than if he were to become his representative. Only mere location may be involved. One footballer can play in a position on the field where another should have played. The first substitutes for the second – 're-placing' him in a depersonalized way, as one piece may be taken from a chess board and another set in its place. A cowardly shepherd may run away and allow the wolf to kill some sheep instead of their owner. It is *to the advantage* of the shepherd that the sheep are killed, but they do not die *on his behalf*. Neither wittingly nor willingly the animals serve as substitutes for the man. No conscious , free and mutual arrangement is made before such a substitution occurs. That can hold true of our first example. One footballer may play in place of another, who – let us imagine – died in an accident on his way to the match.

Representation, however, can only come about through the conscious acceptance by free moral agents on both sides. Someone represents me at a meeting or acts as my legal representative, only when we have agreed that this should be so and that the representation should take place within defined limits. By mutual consent the representative assumes responsibility for a limited period and for limited objectives.

In the case of Christ the agreement from our side takes place only after he has offered amends on our behalf. All the same, individuals have to hear the story of this atonement, react one by one and freely accept what was done for us all. Moreover, they recognize that even Christ's representation has its limits. If St Paul confesses (in language that is unusual for him) that 'Christ lives in me' (Gal. 2. 20), he never maintains, 'Christ believes in me'. Neither Christ nor the Holy Spirit can, properly speaking, represent us in our act of faith as such. Here, as well as elsewhere, representation cannot be unlimited. No one can represent us in believing, hoping and loving.

Besides getting things straight on Christ's role as representative, we should avoid getting into a mess over atonement and *sacrifice*. Two warnings need to be issued.

(A) One expressed or unexpressed supposition has haunted and hurt talk of 'sacrifice': that the sacrificial death of Jesus appeased the divine anger, changed God's mind and drew down on sinful mankind pardon from heaven. Thomas Aquinas, for instance, explains that 'in the proper sense' a sacrifice not only pays 'the honour due to God' but does so, 'in order to placate him'.[14] Such a suggestion stands in remarkable opposition to the

New Testament. God freely *takes the initiative* to re-establish in an enhanced fashion the relationship with man that human sin has broken. His sinful brothers and sisters do not immolate Jesus to propitiate the anger of God and win forgiveness for themselves.

(B) What has just been said should not, however, be perverted into a denial that the events of the first Holy Week constituted a 'sacrifice'. The epistle to the Hebrews, the fathers of the church, the Council of Trent, the Protestant Reformers and many other witnesses to the Christian message have used that term, albeit with significant differences. There should be no call to mount some special rescue operation to keep the language of sacrifice alive. Nevertheless, this language has its difficulties, as an attentive reading of St Paul suggests.

The apostle introduces traditional phraseology about the sacrificial quality of the crucifixion. In the course of his polemic against their immorality, he reminds his Corinthian converts: 'Christ, our paschal lamb, has been sacrificed' (I Cor. 5. 7). Later in that letter he recalls the Lord's Supper at which Jesus announced, 'This cup is the new covenant in my blood' (11. 25). Elsewhere he writes of 'Christ Jesus, whom God put forward as an expiation by his blood, to be received by faith' (Rom. 3. 24f.). The language of sacrifice does flame out here and there in the apostle's letters – unlike the Suffering Servant imagery. (He seems indifferent to, or even unaware of, that imagery.) However, Paul fails to make much of the crucifixion either (*a*) as an *expiatory sacrifice*, or (*b*) as a *sacrifice which brings a new covenant* with God. One can spot the fundamental reasons for this inhibition. The apostle takes the death of Jesus to be an act of God which carries beneficial consequences for men. It was God who 'put forward' his Son to expiate human sins and to usher in the 'new covenant'. Once we see the crucifixion as an act of God towards mankind, we can hardly turn round and speak of God sacrificing to himself. Likewise, any stress on Calvary's consequences 'for us' tends to exclude the theme of its consequences 'for God' and hence its sacrificial quality. Paul knows the cross to be an effect of God's saving will, not its cause. And that belief restrains the apostle's readiness to proclaim Good Friday as an atoning sacrifice which establishes a new relationship between God and man.

Two words gather together Paul's key convictions about Christ's role in the crucifixion: obedience towards his Father and suffering undertaken 'for us'. In loving submission Christ 'became obedient unto death' (Phil. 2. 8). This was a death 'for us'

(Gal. 3. 13) in two senses: he acted as our representative and to our (enormous) advantage.

(3) Mankind misrepresented

We have noted ways in which the roles of God and Christ in affecting the atonement have been misrepresented. Various misunderstandings have lent support to the conventional polemic against the belief that the crucifixion made amends for human sin. A final difficulty to be faced here concerns human involvement. Does belief in atonement (i) fail to produce a sense of commitment and (ii) suggest a world that smells of masochism? As regards (i), talk of atonement seems to bypass practice and simply recall with reverent faith the amends made centuries ago by our representative. Or – and here (ii) goes to the other extreme – expiation looks as if it encourages a sick involvement with Calvary by calling for orgies of self-inflicted pain. Where atonement is understood that way, many people will have none of it. It seems to stress the terrible, if obscure, malice of human sin to the point of supporting excesses of voluntary penance calculated to set right a disturbed world.

In the face of these charges there is no need to twist about like a liar strangling in a web of his fictions. We should admit without fuss that theologies of atonement can go wildly astray. As we have noted, they may even topple over into believing in a punishing God whose anger we must propitiate.

Nevertheless, healthy atonement theology invites well-founded *action* and *acceptance*. Just as the reconciliation and liberation brought by Christ impels believers to act in genuinely reconciling and liberating ways, so the atonement he made on our behalf should alert us to our responsibility for the good state of the moral order. To go back to our diagram. If objective guilt distressingly recalls the infectious damage caused by sin, we can appreciate the other side of the coin – man's duty to uphold the objective moral health of his world. At the level of *action* we cannot distinguish in any final way between the event of atonement and our response to it. We can likewise be drawn into this event through *accepted* (not self-inflicted) suffering. Such accepted suffering can purify and renew a damaged world. It may also witness to a situation where God's power will be made perfect in human weakness.

A Death for All

This chapter began by recalling the conviction St Paul shares with his fellow believers that Christ died 'for all'. Such a notion of representative solidarity strikes the minds of some people and reverberates. A Chinese proverb declares: 'The right man sitting in his house thinking the right thought will be heard five hundred miles distant.' Likewise the right man hanging on his cross for the right cause will save men and women to the end of human history. But this inter-connectedness of all things with a crucifixion two thousand years ago seems unimaginable to other people. Their misgivings deserve a hearing.

We began this book by exploring the *particular* way Jesus went to his death. We tried to assess his intentions, looked at some historical events that occurred during his ministry, and reflected on the specific circumstances that led to the crucifixion. *This* Jewish man spoke with a Galilean accent, wore hair of a definite length and colour, preached like a rabbi of his day (albeit a highly unusual one), and died by a form of torture killing in vogue at that time. Then in his death and resurrection he was believed to have burst through the normal boundaries of history to enjoy a saving influence over the entire story of man and his world. The individual Jesus became the Christ of universal value. Believers called themselves Christians rather than Nazarenes. When they introduced titles like saviour, redeemer, reconciler and liberator, they called Jesus Christ *the* saviour, *the* redeemer, *the* reconciler and *the* liberator. They acknowledged that he had saved all, redeemed all, reconciled all and liberated all. But how could one individual pass through a *specific* set of historical events and achieve such a *universal* effect?

Here it is not enough to point out that Jesus identified himself with all human beings in their basic need for food, lodging and affectionate care (Matt. 25. 31–46). Christian belief maintained not only that he is everyman, but that he was and remains everyman's saviour. Jesus pressed beyond the stage of identifying himself with all to liberate and reconcile all through his death and resurrection.

Here it is not enough to point out that Jesus identified himself with all human beings in their basic need for food, lodging Jesus pressed beyond the stage of identifying himself with all to liberate and reconcile all through his death and resurrection.

How then can one throw light on the universal meaning of the crucifixion of Jesus – taken together with his life and resurrection? A variety of useful answers present themselves. There is no such thing as *the* theological position here. Different writers throw windows open on at least three main perspectives, each of which allows us to glimpse something of value. At the risk of distorting these perspectives, we can group them under the headings of (1) God's role, (2) universal history, and (3) corporate personality. We can summarize these themes in turn.

(1) God's role

In chapter IV we argued that as an 'act of God' the crucifixion indicated a special divine presence and activity. In that death God engaged himself to a special degree and showed his hand decisively. Instead of introducing such 'act of God' terminology, some theologians prefer other ways of linking Calvary with the divinity. Thus Dorothee Sölle described the crucified Christ as representing the absent God.

> Christ took over God's role in the world, but in the process it was changed into the role of the helpless God. The absent God whom Christ represents is the God who is helpless in this world . . . In his last letters, Dietrich Bonhoeffer spoke often of this helplessness of God in the world . . . God allows himself to be edged out of the world and on to the cross. God is weak and powerless in the world, and that is exactly the way, the only way, in which he can be with us and help us. . . . The Bible directs him [sc. man] to the powerlessness and suffering of God; only a suffering God can help.[15]

Whether we refer to Calvary as an 'act of God', speak of Christ as representing God in the world, talk directly of Christ's own divinity, or declare that 'only a suffering God can help', we propose a perspective which readily implies that the crucifixion has universal consequences: the God of all the world is involved in the violent death of Jesus.

(2) Universal history

Wolfhart Pannenberg has popularized another way of appreciating the ultimate and universal significance found in the events of Good Friday and Easter Sunday. What happened to Jesus was not an isolated, if uniquely great, privilege granted to one noble individual after his vicious victimization, but the beginning of the end of all history. The future general resurrection is nothing less than the final and necessary consequence of God's act in raising the crucified Jesus to new life. 'Jesus's resurrection', Pannenberg writes, 'constituted . . . the beginning of the universal resurrection of the dead and the end of the world.'[16]

Whether we embrace Pannenberg's total system or develop our argument another way, we can share his key conviction. Through the resurrection of the dead Jesus the end of all history has already flared forth. The fate which swept him from the scene of visible history made him the first to enter into that final state which all human beings are called.

(3) Corporate personality

St Paul offers a third means for elucidating the universal status which Jesus attained through his dying and rising. He became an 'inclusive personality'. C. F. D. Moule[17] and others rightly interpret the Pauline 'in Christ' along such universalizing lines. Like the apostle the first believers acknowledged themselves to be incorporated into Christ – now understood in more than individual terms. The events of Good Friday and Easter Sunday had driven the early Christians to assess their Lord as a supra-individual who stood larger than life, even though the resurrection did not entail the annihilation of the particular reality which was Jesus of Nazareth. The risen Christ did not identify himself by saying: 'I come in the place of Jesus', or 'I was Jesus', but simply, 'It is I myself'. Despite the uniquely massive transformation involved, the resurrection did not replace Jesus with someone else. Nevertheless, Christians recognized that he now functioned as an inclusive personality, a being of cosmic significance into whom all the baptized knew themselves to be incorporated. During the ministry no disciple understood himself to be 'in Jesus'. But after the death and resurrection believers knew themselves to be 'in Christ' – the object of their faith and hope. 'In Christ', Paul declared, 'all shall be made alive' (I Cor. 15. 22; cf. Rom. 8. 1; Phil. 3. 8f.).

However we care to express the universal impact of the crucifixion, each of the three approaches outlined does more than credit Jesus with offering the noblest example in the style of some super-Socrates. The Athenian philosopher-martyr died in a sense 'for others'. The moral effect of his death encouraged later men and women to endorse the cause of truth, even to the point of being ready to lose their lives for it. Individuals could read the story of Socrates and react by deciding to imitate such dedication to virtue. Nevertheless, Socrates represented no one – let alone

God – in his martyrdom. Through his death he did not gloriously anticipate the final destiny to which all human beings are called. Nor was he believed to become an inclusive personality, so that later adherents of the Socratic method could speak of their being 'in Socrates'.

If Jesus resembled the old philosopher in loyalty to his vocation, he went far beyond him in exemplifying that loyalty. It was not a quiet death by hemlock but a slow and sadistic form of public execution which lay at the end of the road. But merely appealing to the moral example given does not take us far enough in establishing the universal consequences of the crucifixion or any other martyrdom. The example of even the most heroic martyr can enjoy no effect on those who lived and died *before* his day came. Those who come after him can only react one by one to his story – *if* they hear it. It seems impossible to argue for truly universal significance, if we remain merely on the level of moral effects. Add too the fact that effective example can be drawn from allegories like Bunyan's *Pilgrim's Progress* or parables like that of the Good Samaritan. Our moral models do not need to be historical figures like Jesus and Socrates. In brief, even noble examples of virtue will neither have a universal impact, nor will they necessarily derive from real figures of history.

One final observation. In elucidating the universal implications of Calvary we should avoid being high on the belief of the early church but low on the intentions of Jesus himself. Chapter IV pointed to an implicit soteriology already found in his ministry and preaching. This partly anticipated the explicit doctrines of salvation developed by the early Christians. Likewise the *universal* value of Jesus' life, death and resurrection was not simply a post-Easter discovery. Admittedly Jesus confined his ministry to Palestine and Jewish audiences. Nevertheless, he addressed them as men and women, healed and helped them in their basic human needs, and forgave the sins which blighted their lives as God's sons and daughters. The preaching of Jesus implied a unique claim to authority – and not just an authority restricted to Israel itself. When he maintained that one's attitude towards him would carry eternal consequences, he addressed that warning to everyone and not simply to every Jew: 'Everyone who acknowledges me before men, the Son of man also will acknowledge before the angels of God; but he who denies me before men will be denied before the angels of God' (Luke 12. 8f.). To sum up. Back in the ministry of Jesus we can spot an implicit universality.

In the light of the crucifixion and resurrection St Paul and other early Christians explicitly recognized that what Jesus had done and suffered was done and suffered 'for all'.

A PERSONAL EPILOGUE

Beyond question the execution of Jesus lodges in the mind of man as no other death has. We can all look at this crucifixion, think about this crucifixion and talk about this crucifixion. Nevertheless, we may be looking, thinking and talking from very different points of view.

My book has reflected on three dimensions of the crucifixion: the story of Jesus' road to Calvary, the agents of his execution and the results of his death. In exploring the history, the causes and the consequences of Good Friday, I am sure to have been defective in perspective and procedure at many points. But at least I have tried to avoid embracing all the stock versions and threadbare theologies of the cross. Too often belief in the crucified Christ gives ground to evasive tendencies, conventional reactions creep in, and dull language grinds on. If I have found and fashioned ways of reflecting on the crucifixion which let it speak again with fresh power to a few people, I am grateful.

To conclude. This book has concentrated on Jesus' crucifixion and said little about our own death and dying. Yet we are bound to him both through a mysterious fellowship in suffering, and through our terror at the approach of death. Not love but death appears to conquer all. *Mors vincit omnia*. We cannot deal with this sense of hollow meaninglessness by appealing to life – even by recalling that 'the glory of God is man fully alive'. The glory of God was once a wounded man who stumbled, fell and became fully dead. Only the willingness to accept our broken hopes and let ourselves die with that man can make full and final sense of our lives.

NOTES

INTRODUCTION

1. *Form criticism* isolates and analyses the smallest independent units on which the gospels drew. By stressing the role of the early church in transmitting, modifying and creating these units of tradition, form criticism leaves us with the task of assessing the historical facts which lie behind the tradition. *Redaction criticism* examines the work of the evangelists in editing the materials inherited from the community. It overlaps with *composition criticism*. This analyses the contents of a gospel in the setting which occasioned its composition, as well as exploring the objectives the author had in mind.

2. Ulrich Simon, 'The Multidimensional Picture of Jesus', *What about the New Testament?*, ed., M. D. Hooker and C. J. Hickling, SCM Press 1975, p. 116.

3. Jürgen Moltmann, *The Crucified God*, trans., R. A. Wilson and J. S. Bowden, SCM Press 1974, p. 186.

I. JESUS THE MARTYR

1. Homer, *Iliad*, trans., E. V. Rieu, Penguin Books 1950, Book X, 77–85, p. 399.

2. *Iliad*, Book VI, 429–32, Rieu, p. 128.

3. From an unpublished paper of Rev. Michael J. Buckley, SJ, 'A Letter to the Ordinands'.

4. R. W. Chambers, *Thomas More*, first edition, London 1935, reprinted 1962, p. 347.

5. Ibid., pp. 350f.

II. JESUS ON THE RUN

1. Kierkegaard, *Philosophical Fragments*, Princeton 1936, p. 130.

2. Josephus, *Antiquities*, 18, iv, 1–2.

3. Here I use the New English Bible. The RSV weakens the sense of the original: 'His friends . . . went out to seize him, for they said, "He is beside himself".'

4. *If* the beloved disciple were a cousin, he would make the third relative present – alongside Jesus' mother and an aunt.

5. Piet Schoonenberg, 'The Kenosis or Self Emptying of Christ', *Concilium*, vol. 1, no. 2, January 1966, p. 35.

6. Plato, *Phaedo*, trans., R. S. Bluck, Routledge & Kegan Paul 1955, 63E, 64A, pp. 46f.

7. *Angelus Silesius. Pèlerin cherubinique*, trans., H. Plard, Paris 1946, IV. 107.

8. 'For this reason the Father loves me, because I lay down my life, that I may take it again. No one takes it from me, but I lay it down of my own accord' (John 10. 17f.).

9. These three texts run as follows: 'As Moses lifted up the serpent in the wilderness, so must the Son of man be lifted up' (3. 14). 'When you have lifted up the Son of man, then you will know that I am he, and that I do nothing of my own authority but speak thus as the Father taught me' (8. 28). ' "And I, when I am lifted up from the earth, will draw all men to myself." He said this to show by what death he was to die' (12. 32–33). Only the third text expressly identifies the 'lifting up' with the coming crucifixion. By leaving the term vague in the earlier passages, John softens the feeling of an inexorable movement to violent death.

10. *Antiquities*, 18, v, 2.

11. Hammarskjöld, *Markings*, trans., W. H. Auden and L. Sjöberg, Faber & Faber, 1964, p. 31.

12. *The Poetical Works of Robert Herrick*, ed. F. W. Moorman, London 1921–51, p. 308.

13. Peter Gallwey, *The Watches of the Passion*, London 1894, vol. II, pp. 25–26.

14. *Markings*, p. 33.

III. CRUCIFIED

1. Ulrich Simon, 'The Multidimensional Picture of Jesus', *What about the New Testament?*, p. 121.

2. See my *The Theology of Secularity*, Dublin 1974. Paul Winter remarks about Jesus himself: 'Religion without politics was equally unthinkable to him as politics without religion . . . In Jesus' thought, as generally in Jewish thought, religion and politics are inseparable', *On the Trial of Jesus*, second edition, Berlin 1974, note 19, p. 69; hereafter referred to as *Trial*.

3. As in Mark, Jesus at once refers to the Son of man: 'But I tell you, hereafter you will see the Son of man seated at the right hand of Power, and coming on the clouds of heaven' (26. 64; cf. Mark 14. 62).

4. W. R. Wilson, *The Execution of Jesus*, Charles Scribner's Sons, New York 1970; hereafter referred to as *Execution*. Wilson rightly insists that his 'book is not a devotional treatise but an analytical one. The religious significance of the death of Jesus is not the issue here' (p. x).

5. C. H. Dodd, *The Interpretation of the Fourth Gospel*, Cambridge University Press 1953, p. 357.

6. *Execution*, p. 2.

7. Ibid., p. 200.

8. *Nietzsche*, trans., W. Kaufmann, third edition, New York 1968, pp. 338f.

9. *Execution*, pp. 169f., italics mine.

10. Ibid., p. 201.

11. Ibid., pp. 172f., italics mine.

12. *Trial*, p. 59; quoted and endorsed by Wilson, *Execution*, p. 196.

13. *Execution*, p. 132. Wilson here denies that we should use such terms to describe the priests' opposition to Jesus.

14. Ibid., p. 122.

IV. AGENTS OF THE CRUCIFIXION

1. In a (so far) unpublished manuscript on the problem of evil.
2. *Antichrist*, no. 7.
3. Raymond Williams, *Modern Tragedy*, Chatto & Windus 1966, p. 160.
4. Paul Winter, *Trial*, p. 200.
5. II Maccabees 7. 37ff.; IV Maccabees 1. 11; 6. 29; 9. 23f.; 17. 22 etc. Admittedly IV Maccabees *may* have received its final form as late as AD 100. But II Maccabees certainly predates Jesus.
6. *Modern Tragedy*, note 1, p. 195.
7. See Mark 14. 10; Luke 22. 48; John 18. 5 etc.
8. Aquinas, *Summa Theologica*, III, qu. 47, a. 3.

V. THE UNCRUCIFIED IS THE UNHEALED

1. Williams, *Modern Tragedy*, p. 157.
2. See Matt. 23. 29f.
3. See my 'Power made Perfect in Weakness: II Cor. 12. 9–10', *Catholic Biblical Quarterly*, 33, 1971, pp. 528–37.
4. E. S. Fiorenza, 'Redemption as Liberation: Apoc. 1. 5f. and 5. 9f.', *Catholic Biblical Quarterly*, 36, 1974, pp. 228–29, italics mine.
5. See the apostolic exhortation by Pope Paul VI on 'reconciliation within the church', 8 December 1974.
6. In what follows I must acknowledge my debt to T. Michael McNulty, the co-author with me of 'St Paul and the Language of Reconciliation', *Colloquium*, 6, 1973, pp. 3–8.
7. Gustaf Aulén, *Christus Victor*, trans., A. G. Herbert, London 1931; New York 1951 and SPCK 1970 edition p. 146.
8. Ibid., p. 149.
9. G. D. Kaufmann, *Systematic Theology: A Historical Perspective*, New York 1968, note, p. 389.
10. 'Pauline Theology', *Jerome Biblical Commentary*, ed., R. E. Brown et al., Prentice Hall 1968 and Cassell Collier Macmillan 1969, II, p. 814, italics mine.

VI. ATONEMENT FOR ALL

1. *Cur Deus Homo*, I. 15, trans., S. N. Deane, Chicago 1930, p. 210.
2. Calvin, *Institutes*, II, 16; trans., J. Allen, Grand Rapids 1949, I, p. 553.
3. From Bossuet, *Nouveau Cours de Méditations* etc., cited in Philippe de la Trinité, *What is Redemption?*, trans., A. Armstrong, Burns & Oates 1963, pp. 22–23.
4. Bossuet, *Devotion to the Blessed Virgin*, trans., F. M. Capes, London 1899, p. 122.
5. Barth, *Church Dogmatics*, T. & T. Clark 1957, II/2, p. 758.
6. D. Bonhoeffer to E. Bethge, 18 July 1944, *Letters and Papers from Prison*, enlarged edition, trans., R. Fuller, et al., SCM Press 1971, p. 361.
7. Moran, *The Present Revelation*, New York 1972, pp. 278f.; 282f.
8. Baum, *Man Becoming*, New York 1970, p. 223; cf., pp. 221ff.
9. See further S. Legasse, 'À propos de l'idée de substitution pénale dans la Rédemption. Note exegetique', *Bulletin de Littérature Ecclésiastique*, 69, 1968, pp. 81–97; on Romans see E. Käsemann, *An die Römer*, second edition, Tübingen 1974, pp. 203ff.
10. Luke 3. 7; John 3. 36; Romans 1. 18f., etc.

11. G. Kittel (ed.), *Theological Dictionary of the New Testament*, V, p. 422.

12. Hebrews introduces sacrificial imagery. But it is by no means clear that either Isaiah 53 (despite v. 10 which speaks of 'an offering for sin') or Mark 10. 45 *must* be interpreted in a context of cult. Giving one's life on behalf of others can obviously happen quite apart from any formal sitting of liturgical sacrifice.

13. To preclude any misunderstanding, let me remark that I am well aware the IV Maccabees does not belong to the canon of the Bible (even for Roman Catholics!), and may have been finally composed as late as AD 100. Nevertheless, this book reflects the ideas that were already established by the time of Jesus.

14. *Summa Theologica*, III, qu. 48, a. 3, resp.

15. Dorothee Sölle, *Christ the Representative*, trans., D. Lewis, SCM Press 1967, p. 150.

16. Pannenberg, *Jesus – God and Man*, SCM Press 1968, p. 106.

17. C. F. D. Moule, *The Phenomenon of the New Testament*, SCM Press 1967, pp. 21–42.

VERY SELECT BIBLIOGRAPHY

(ET = English translation)

Alzeghy, Z. and Flick, M., *Sussidio Bibliografico per una Teologia della Croce*, Rome 1975.

Banks, R. (ed.), *Reconciliation and Hope*, Paternoster Press 1974.

Dillistone, F. W., *The Christian Understanding of the Atonement*, Nisbet 1968.

Dupont, J., *La Réconciliation dans la théologie de saint Paul*, Paris 1952.

Franks, R. S., *The Work of Christ*, Nelson 1962.

Galot, J., *La Rédemption, Mystère d'Alliance*, Paris 1965.

Hodgson, L., *The Doctrine of the Atonement*, Nisbet 1951.

Käsemann, E., 'The Pauline Theology of the Cross', *Interpretation*, 24, 1970, pp. 151–77.

Kasper, W., *Jesus der Christus*, Mainz 1974.

Kessler, H., *Die theologische Bedeutung des Todes Jesu*, Düsseldorf 1970.

Klappert, B., *Die Auferweckung des Gekreuzigten*, Neukirchen 1971.

Klappert, B. (ed.), *Diskussion um Kreuz und Auferstehung*, Wuppertal 1967.

Knox, J., *The Death of Christ*, Collins/Fontana 1959.

Küng, H., *Christ Sein*, Munich 1974.

Lohse, E., *History of the Suffering and Death of Jesus Christ*, ET, Philadelphia 1967.

Lyonnet, S. (with Sabourin, L.), *Sin, Redemption and Sacrifice*, Rome 1970.

Moltmann, J., *The Crucified God*, ET, SCM Press 1974.

Mozley, J. K., *The Doctrine of the Atonement*, Duckworth 1915.

Müller, U. B., 'Die Bedeutung des Kreuzestodes Jesu im Johannes-evangelium', *Kerygma und Dogma*, 21, 1975, pp. 49–71.

North, R., 'Yom Kippur and the jubilee year of reconciliation', *Theology Digest*, 22, 1974, pp. 346–59.

Pannenberg, W., *Jesus – God and Man*, ET, SCM Press 1968.

Philippe de la Trinité, *What is the Redemption?*, Burns & Oates 1963.

Rahner, K., et al., 'Salvation', *Sacramentum Mundi*, 5, pp. 405–38.

Rivière, J., 'Rédemption', *Dictionnaire de Théologie Catholique*, 13, col. 1912–2004.

Young, F. M., *Sacrifice and the Death of Christ*, SPCK 1975.

INDEX OF NAMES

Achilles, 3, 5
Angelus Silesius, 28, 117
Anselm, 75, 94, 101
Aquinas, Thomas, 22f., 59, 67, 94, 107, 118
Arthur, King, 3, 5f.
Athanasius, 74
Auden, W. H., 65, 117
Aulén, Gustaf, 82, 83, 101, 118

Barth, Karl, 82, 95, 101, 118
Baum, Gregory, 96f., 118
Becket, Thomas, 20
Boethius, 10f.
Bonhoeffer, Dietrich, 10f., 12, 14, 35, 51, 52, 95, 118
Bossuet, J. B., 94f., 96, 118
Browne, Sir Thomas, 1, 93
Buckley, Michael J., 116
Bultmann, Rudolf, 101

Caiaphas, 20, 25, 34, 41f., 43f., 51f., 53, 64, 65f., 69, 72
Calvin, J., 94, 96, 118
Chambers, R. W., 116
Clitherow, Margaret, 10, 45
Cowburn, John, 58
Cranmer, Thomas, 12, 35

Dillistone, F. W., ix, 120
Dodd, C. H., 117
Dostoyevsky, Fëdor, 70

Eliot, T. S., 61, 70

Fiorenza, E. S., 78f., 118
Fitzmyer, Joseph A., 87
Francis of Assisi, 39
Freud, Sigmund, 28

Gallwey, Peter, 38, 117
Gandhi, Mohandas, 7f., 9f.
Goethe, Johann Wolfgang von, 40

Hammarskjöld, Dag, 35, 39, 117
Hector, 3f., 5
Henry VIII, King, 11, 13, 36, 51
Herod Antipas, 20, 22, 24f., 33f., 43, 45
Herrick, Robert, 38, 117
Hitler, Adolf, 11, 16, 51
Homer, 1, 116
Huss, John, 10, 14

Ignatius of Antioch, 10, 12

Joan of Arc, 10f., 14, 35f., 51
John the Baptist, 8, 24f., 26, 30f., 33f., 43, 44
Josephus, 34, 116
Judas, x, 6, 25, 41, 52, 64, 65f., 67f., 69

Käsemann, Ernst, 89, 118, 120
Kaufman, Gordon D., 86, 118
Kennedy, John F., 7f., 9
Kierkegaard, Søren, 21, 116
King, Martin Luther, 7f.

Legasse, S., 118
Luther, Martin, 16, 18

McKenzie, John L., 96
McNulty, T. Michael, 118
Marx, Karl, 17, 70
Miller, Arthur, 58
Moltmann, Jürgen, ix, xii, 116, 120
Moran, Gabriel, 95f., 118
More, Thomas, 10f., 12, 13f., 35f., 45, 51, 116
Moses, 22, 31, 45, 63, 81
Moule, C. F. D., 112, 119

Nelson, Horatio, 3, 5f., 7, 9
Nietzsche, Friedrich, 16, 40, 47, 59f., 117

O'Collins, Gerald, 117

Pannenberg, Wolfhart, 117f., 119, 120
Paul VI, Pope, 82, 118
Pilate, 5f., 12, 17, 19f., 21f., 25, 34, 41, 44, 45, 47f., 49, 50, 51f., 53, 60, 64, 65f., 69, 72
Plato, xi, 12f., 45, 117
Plunkett, Oliver, 10, 11

Rahner, Karl, 55, 120
Ridley, Nicholas, 10, 11, 14
Roper, Margaret, 14

Savonarola, 10f., 14
Schoonenberg, Piet, 26, 116
Schweitzer, Albert, 17
Shakespeare, William, 105
Simon, Ulrich, xii, 40, 116, 117
Socrates, xi, 10, 12f., 15, 27f., 35f., 45, 52, 57, 112f.,
Sölle, Dorothee, 111, 119
Stählin, Gustav, 98

Taylor, Vincent, 92
Thomas à Kempis, 28, 56
Tyrell, George, 38

Venantius Fortunatus, 4

Williams, Raymond, 61, 65f., 70, 118
Wilson, William R., 44, 46–51, 117
Winter, Paul, 48f., 50, 117, 118
Wittgenstein, Ludwig, 86f.